Where Two or Three Are Gathered

Music from *Psallite* by
The Collegeville Composers Group

LITURGICAL PRESS
Collegeville, Minnesota

www.litpress.org
800.858.5450

Dedicated to
Fr. Nicholas Doub, O.S.B.,
27 February 1949–4 December 2002,
who inspired this work

ACKNOWLEDGEMENTS

The twenty-five titles contained in this edition are taken from a larger collection published by Liturgical Press entitled *Psallite: Sacred Song for Liturgy and Life,* Year A, with an Imprimatur from ✠ Most Reverend John F. Kinney, Diocese of Saint Cloud in Minnesota, June 15, 2007.

Music from *Psallite: Sacred Song for Liturgy and Life,* © 2005, 2006, 2007 by The Collegeville Composers Group (Carol Browning, Catherine Christmas, Cyprian Consiglio, O.S.B. Cam., Paul F. Ford, Ph.D., Paul Inwood). All rights reserved. Published and administered by Liturgical Press, Collegeville, Minnesota 56321.

Antiphon texts and the texts of *Light of the World* and *The Word of God at Work in Us* from *Psallite: Sacred Song for Liturgy and Life,* © 2005, 2006, 2007 by The Collegeville Composers Group (Carol Browning, Catherine Christmas, Cyprian Consiglio, O.S.B. Cam., Paul F. Ford, Ph.D., Paul Inwood). All rights reserved. Published and administered by Liturgical Press, Collegeville, Minnesota 56321.

The Psalm texts are from The Grail (England), © 1963, 1986, 1993, 2000, The Grail. All rights reserved. Licensed for *Where Two or Three Are Gathered* and reprinted by permission of GIA Publications, Inc., agent. *Imprimatur:* ✠ Most Reverend William Keeler, President, National Conference of Catholic Bishops, September 12, 1993.

The Canticle texts are from the New Revised Standard Version (NRSV) Bible, © 1989, Division of Christian Education of the National Council of the Churches of Christ in the United States of America. All rights reserved. Used with permission. *Imprimatur:* ✠ Most Reverend Daniel E. Pilarczyk, President, National Conference of Catholic Bishops, September 12, 1991.

The cover design is by James Rhoades; photograph by Janie Airey, Digital Vision.

© 2007 by Order of Saint Benedict, Collegeville, Minnesota. All rights reserved. No part of this book may be reproduced in any form, by print, microfilm, microfiche, mechanical recording, photocopying, translation, or by any other means, known or yet unknown, for any purpose except brief quotations in reviews and as noted on page five, without the previous written permission of Liturgical Press, Saint John's Abbey, P.O. Box 7500, Collegeville, Minnesota 56321-7500. Printed in the United States of America.

ISBN 978-0-8146-3077-8

Contents

Now Is the Hour 6
  First Sunday of Advent, Year A
  Song for the Table

Be Patient, Beloved 8
  Third Sunday of Advent, Year A
  Song for the Table

Let the King of Glory Come In 12
  Fourth Sunday of Advent, Year A
  Song for the Word

Jesus, Mighty Lord, Come Save Us 14
  Fourth Sunday of Advent, Year A
  Song for the Table

Clothed in Christ, One in Christ 16
  Baptism of the Lord, Year A—Song for the Table
  Easter Vigil—Baptismal Acclamation

Give Us Living Water 18
  Third Sunday of Lent, Year A
  Song for the Table

Give Thanks to the Lord, Alleluia 20
  Second Sunday of Easter, Year A
  Song for the Word

At Your Word Our Hearts Are Burning 21
  Third Sunday of Easter, Year A
  Song for the Table

I Am the Way: Follow Me 22
  Fifth Sunday of Easter, Year A
  Song for the Table

Here I Am 24
  Second Sunday in Ordinary Time, Year A
  Song for the Word

Light of the World 25
  Third Sunday in Ordinary Time, Year A
  Song for the Table

In God Alone Is My Soul at Rest 28
  Eighth Sunday in Ordinary Time, Year A
  Song for the Word

Keep These Words in Your Heart and Soul 29
  Ninth Sunday in Ordinary Time, Year A
  Song for the Table

Love Is My Desire 30
  Tenth Sunday in Ordinary Time, Year A
  Song for the Table

The Mercy of God Is for All 33
  Twentieth Sunday in Ordinary Time, Year A
  Song for the Table

Everlasting Is Your Love 36
  Twenty-first Sunday in Ordinary Time, Year A
  Song for the Word

All Things Are from the Lord 38
  Twenty-first Sunday in Ordinary Time, Year A
  Song for the Table

Where Two or Three Are Gathered 40
  Twenty-third Sunday in Ordinary Time, Year A
  Song for the Table

Lord, You Are Close 42
  Twenty-fifth Sunday in Ordinary Time, Year A
  Song for the Word

Remember, Lord 44
  Twenty-sixth Sunday in Ordinary Time, Year A
  Song for the Word

All That Is True 46
  Twenty-seventh Sunday in Ordinary Time, Year A
  Song for the Table

I Shall Dwell in the House of the Lord 49
  Twenty-eighth Sunday in Ordinary Time, Year A
  Song for the Word

The Word of God at Work in Us 50
  Thirty-first Sunday in Ordinary Time, Year A
  Song for the Table

Come, All You Good and Faithful Servants 52
  Thirty-third Sunday in Ordinary Time, Year A
  Song for the Table

A River Flows 56
  The Dedication of the Lateran Basilica, Years ABC
  Song for the Word

Reproducible Graphics 58
  Listed alphabetically by title

INTRODUCTORY NOTES

Where Two or Three Are Gathered is a selection of twenty-five titles from the newest collection of music published by Liturgical Press, *Psallite: Sacred Song for Liturgy and Life*. A new collection of liturgical songs inspired by the antiphons and psalms of the *Roman Missal*, *Psallite* includes music for each Sunday, Solemnity, and major feast day of the liturgical year.

For each liturgy, *Psallite* provides biblically based options for the entrance/opening song (the SONG FOR THE WEEK); the response song during the Liturgy of the Word (the SONG FOR THE WORD); and the song during the Communion procession (the SONG FOR THE TABLE). This collection contains three hundred new biblically based liturgical songs. While the music in this collection suggests specific Sundays or celebrations for its use, they all have various, repeatable uses throughout the liturgical year.

The name *Psallite* (SAH-lee-tay) comes from the Latin version of Psalm 47:8, *psallite sapienter*, "sing praise with all your skill."

Psallite's music connects liturgy and life, church and home. The SONG FOR THE WEEK may be your theme tune for the entire week. The SONG FOR THE WORD may echo in your mind and keep the Word alive in your heart all day. The SONG FOR THE TABLE may be the one that you sing around your own dining table. All this is achieved by means of memorable music that will transform your life. Once this music gets under your skin, there's no turning back.

The SONG FOR THE WEEK opens the celebration, intensifies the unity of the assembly, leads their thoughts to the mystery of the liturgical season or festivity, and accompanies the procession of the presider and ministers. Another option is to use the SONG FOR THE WEEK at the end of the liturgy (with the addition of a doxology) to send forth the assembly into the world.

The SONG FOR THE WORD, an entirely new repertory of short, memorable antiphons, serves as the golden thread of the Liturgy of the Word.

The SONG FOR THE TABLE, which is the heart of *Psallite*, takes its texts and themes from the Liturgy of the Word, especially from the gospel of the day, transformed into processional music. People will now experience that the promises God made in his Word are fulfilled in the body and blood of Christ.

Psallite's music provides flexibility and allows leaders of music ministry to adapt the music for their assemblies. On the one hand, *Psallite* was designed for those parishes with the most limited musical resources: one well-trained cantor, no accompanist, but an assembly eager to sing the Mass. On the other hand, satisfying vocal, keyboard, and guitar arrangements will win the hearts of the most accomplished choirs and instrumentalists. Many of the descants not marked for a specific voice part may be sung in the alto/tenor range as well as the soprano range.

The style of music is eclectic—with influences ranging from chant to Afro-Caribbean to folksong but in all cases essentially vocal. The cantor calls to the assembly and the assembly responds. And every word they sing is biblically based.

The verse tones of *Psallite* can be used with any translation of the psalms, especially any Grail-based translation. Because *Psallite* models the use of moderately inclusive, horizontally inclusive language, it employs the 1993 Grail revision sponsored by the United States Conference of Catholic Bishops with the *imprimatur* of then Bishop now Cardinal William H. Keeler, who was president at that time. The biblical canticles are mostly taken from the New Revised Standard Version, with some original translations for good measure.

Singing the antiphons and psalms of *Psallite* restores psalm-singing as our primary prayer language. Singing this kind of music helps our assemblies find their voices so that we all can sing the Mass, not just sing at Mass. Singing the same antiphons that our sisters and brothers sang at least a thousand years ago, and in some cases nearly two thousand years ago, connects us spiritually to the great communion of saints, a procession in which we are only the most recent walkers. Singing the various styles of music in *Psallite* will also help break down the cultural barriers that keep us from being "one body, one spirit, in Christ."

ABOUT THE COMPOSERS

The Collegeville Composers Group, a team of international musicians working collaboratively to create the collection, composed the music of *Psallite*. The composers group includes:

Carol Browning, the Director of Liturgy and Music at Saint Mary Magdalen Catholic Community in Camarillo, California, and a music minister for almost twenty years. A member of the Religious Society of Friends (Quakers), Carol is a liturgical composer and an independently published inspirational songwriter.

Catherine Christmas, an accomplished organist and choir director, currently studying for a Master's in Pastoral Liturgy at Heythrop College, University of London.

Cyprian Consiglio, O.S.B. Cam., a musician, composer, author, and teacher who is a monk of the Camaldolese Congregation. He spends about half his time at home, writing and composing, and the other half of his time on the road, performing and teaching.

Paul F. Ford, Ph.D., a professor of systematic theology and liturgy, Saint John's Seminary, Camarillo, California. He is the author of *By Flowing Waters: Chant for the Liturgy*, published by Liturgical Press.

Paul Inwood, the Director of Liturgy and Director of Music for the Diocese of Portsmouth, England. He is an internationally known liturgist, composer, organist, choir director, and clinician. His liturgical music appears in numerous hymnals worldwide.

ADDITIONAL RESOURCES

Where Two or Three Are Gathered—CD
This full-length recording includes the 25 titles in the *Where Two or Three Are Gathered* collection.
  978-0-8146-7965-4 $16.95

We Will Follow You, Lord
A collection of 28 titles taken from *Psallite: Sacred Song for Liturgy and Life*, Year C. Titles include: The Days Are Coming, Surely Coming • My Soul Rejoices In God • God's Love Is Revealed To Us • Not on Bread Alone Are We Nourished • You Are My Hiding Place, O Lord • Lord, Cleanse My Heart, Make Me New • People of God, Flock of the Lord • A New Commandment • Joyfully You Will Draw Water • All Who Labor, Come to Me • This Day Is Holy to the Lord Our God • Love Bears All Things • Cast Out into the Deep • Forgive, and You Will Be Forgiven • Speak Your Word, O Lord, and We Shall Be Healed • For You My Soul Is Thirsting, O God, My God • We Will Follow You, Lord • Listen, I Stand At the Door and Knock • Do Not Store Up Earthly Treasures • From the East and West, From the North and South • In Every Age, O Lord, You Have Been Our Refuge • I Am Your Savior, My People • Seek the Lord! Long For the Lord! • Take Hold of Eternal Life • Worthy Is the Lamb Who Was Slain • Let Us Go Rejoicing to the House of the Lord • I Will Praise You, I Will Thank You • I Will Dwell With You, My House a House of Prayer

  Music collection: 978-0-8146-3075-4 $11.95;
    5 or more copies $9.95* each
  CD recording: 978-0-8146-7964-7 $16.95

Walk in My Ways
A collection of 27 titles taken from *Psallite: Sacred Song for Liturgy and Life*, Year B. Titles include: To You, O Lord, I Lift My Soul • Rejoice in the Lord, Again, Rejoice • We Receive from Your Fullness • Here Is My Servant, Here Is My Son • Give, Your Father Sees • Those Who Love Me, I Will Deliver • My Shepherd Is the Lord • There Is Mercy in the Lord • This Is My Body • Send Out Your Spirit • Christ, Our Pasch • Live on in My Love • I Will See You Again • Walk in My Ways • Venite, Adoremus • God Heals the Broken • Lead Me, Guide Me • Here in Your Presence • All You Nations • Don't Be Afraid • Those Who Do Justice • Let the Word Make a Home in Your Heart • I Loved Wisdom More than Health or Beauty • Courage! Get Up! • My Plans for You Are Peace • Rejoice in the Lord on This Feast of the Saints • May God Grant Us Joy of Heart

  Music collection: 978-0-8146-3058-7 $11.95;
    5 or more copies $9.95* each
  CD recording: 978-0-8146-7960-9 $16.95

To order or for further information contact:
Liturgical Press • www.litpress.org • 800.858.5450

Psallite: Sacred Song for Liturgy and Life
Full accompaniment edition.
Published in three volumes, these editions include the full accompaniment and cantor/schola verses for all Sundays, Solemnities and major Feasts of the liturgical cycle. Plastic coil binding, 8½" x 10⅞", approximately 320 pp.

Individual volumes: 1–4 copies, $24.95 each, 5 or more copies, $19.95* net each; please inquire for bulk purchases.
  978-0-8146-3064-8   Year A
  978-0-8146-3059-4   Year B
  978-0-8146-3065-5   Year C

Complete three-volume set (Years ABC): 1–4 sets, $59.95 per set; 5 or more sets, $49.95* net per set.
  978-0-8146-3060-0   Years ABC

Psallite Cantor/Choir Edition
This edition contains cantor/schola descants and harmonies for all Sundays and solemnities of the liturgical year and includes liturgical and Scriptural indices for various uses and planning. Titles are placed in alphabetical order. Single volume contains all titles in the *Psallite* collection.
  978-0-8146-3088-4
Kivar, 504 pp., 7 x 10, 1–4 copies $24.95; 5–9 copies $19.95 net; 10 or more copies $16.95* net

Psallite Antiphons on CD-ROM
Easy-to-use graphic files of all *Psallite* assembly antiphons (Years ABC) that can be used to select and insert music into desktop publishing documents, PowerPoint presentations, or other custom worship aids and programs. The parish or institution is required to purchase an annual reprint license in order to legally reproduce the antiphons.
  978-0-8146-7961-6 $39.95 CD-ROM
  978-0-8146-3061-7 $35.00 Annual license

*Asterisk indicates discount price available only on "no-returns" basis.

Reprint Policy

Before reproducing the assembly graphics on pages 58–64, you must secure the appropriate Reprint License. By using this copyrighted material, you have a moral obligation to the composers whose livelihood depends on receiving a fair compensation for the use of their work. We trust that you value their work and will agree to this requirement. The following Reprint License options are available: 1) the purchase of a $35.00 Annual Reprint License from Liturgical Press (the reporting of titles is not required when reproduced; 2) membership with the licensing service OneLicense.net (you must report the use of titles each time they are reproduced). Each reprint must include the title and the full copyright notice as it appears below the graphic.

Now Is the Hour
First Sunday of Advent, Year A: Song for the Table

Psalm 85:9, 11-14; Isaiah 2:2-5; Romans 13:11; Matthew 24:42, 44

1. I will hear what the Lord God <u>has</u> to say,
   a voice that <u>speaks</u> of peace,
   peace for his people <u>and</u> friends
   and those who turn to God <u>in</u> their hearts.

2. Mercy and faithful<u>ness</u> have met;
   justice and peace <u>have</u> embraced.
   Faithfulness shall spring from <u>the</u> earth
   and justice look <u>down</u> from heaven.

3. The Lord will <u>make</u> us prosper
   and our earth shall <u>yield</u> its fruit.
   Justice shall march in <u>the</u> forefront,
   and peace shall fol<u>low</u> the way.

4. In days to come
   the mountain <u>of</u> the Lord's house
   shall be established as the highest <u>of</u> the mountains,
   and shall be raised above <u>the</u> hills;
   all the na<u>tions</u> shall stream to it.

5. Many peoples shall <u>come</u> and say,
   "Come, let us go up to the mountain of the Lord,
   to the house of the <u>God</u> of Jacob;
   that he may teach us <u>his</u> ways
   and that we may walk <u>in</u> his paths."

Now Is the Hour, pg. 2

Verse Tone

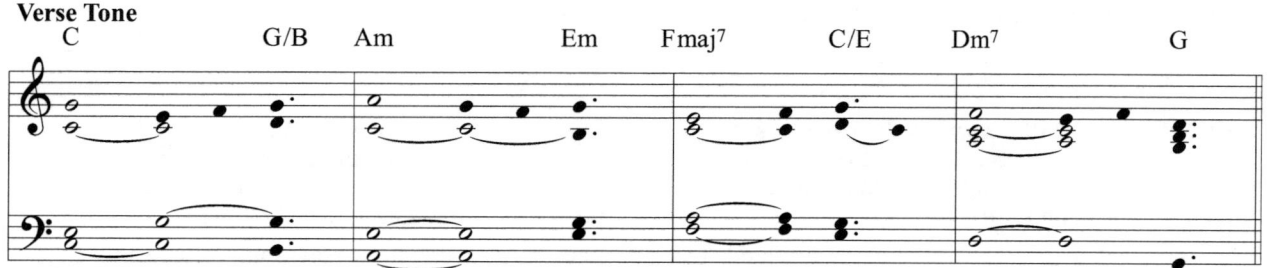

6. The LORD shall judge be<u>tween</u> the nations,
   and shall arbitrate for <u>many</u> peoples;
   they shall beat their swords in<u>to</u> plowshares,
   and their spears <u>into</u> pruning hooks.

7. Nation shall not lift up sword a<u>gainst</u> nation,
   neither shall they learn war <u>any</u> more.
   O house of Ja<u>cob</u>, come,
   let us walk in the light <u>of</u> the LORD!

8. You know what <u>time</u> it is,
   how it is now the moment for you to <u>wake</u> from sleep.
   For salvation is nearer to <u>us</u> now
   than when we be<u>came</u> believers.

9. Therefore <u>keep</u> awake,
   for you do not know on what day your <u>Lord</u> is coming.
   Therefore you also must <u>be</u> ready,
   for the Son of Man is coming at an unex<u>pect</u>ed hour.

Performance Notes
The Antiphon melody is derived from the old French carol tune "Shepherds, shake off your drowsy sleep."

Psalm text: The Grail (England), © 1963, 1986, 1993, 2000, The Grail, GIA Publications, Inc., agent. All rights reserved. Used with permission.
Canticle text: NRSV Bible, © 1989, Division of Christian Education of the National Council of the Churches of Christ in the United States of America. All rights reserved.
Music and antiphon text: © 2007, The Collegeville Composers Group. All rights reserved. Published and administered by the Liturgical Press, Collegeville, MN 56321.

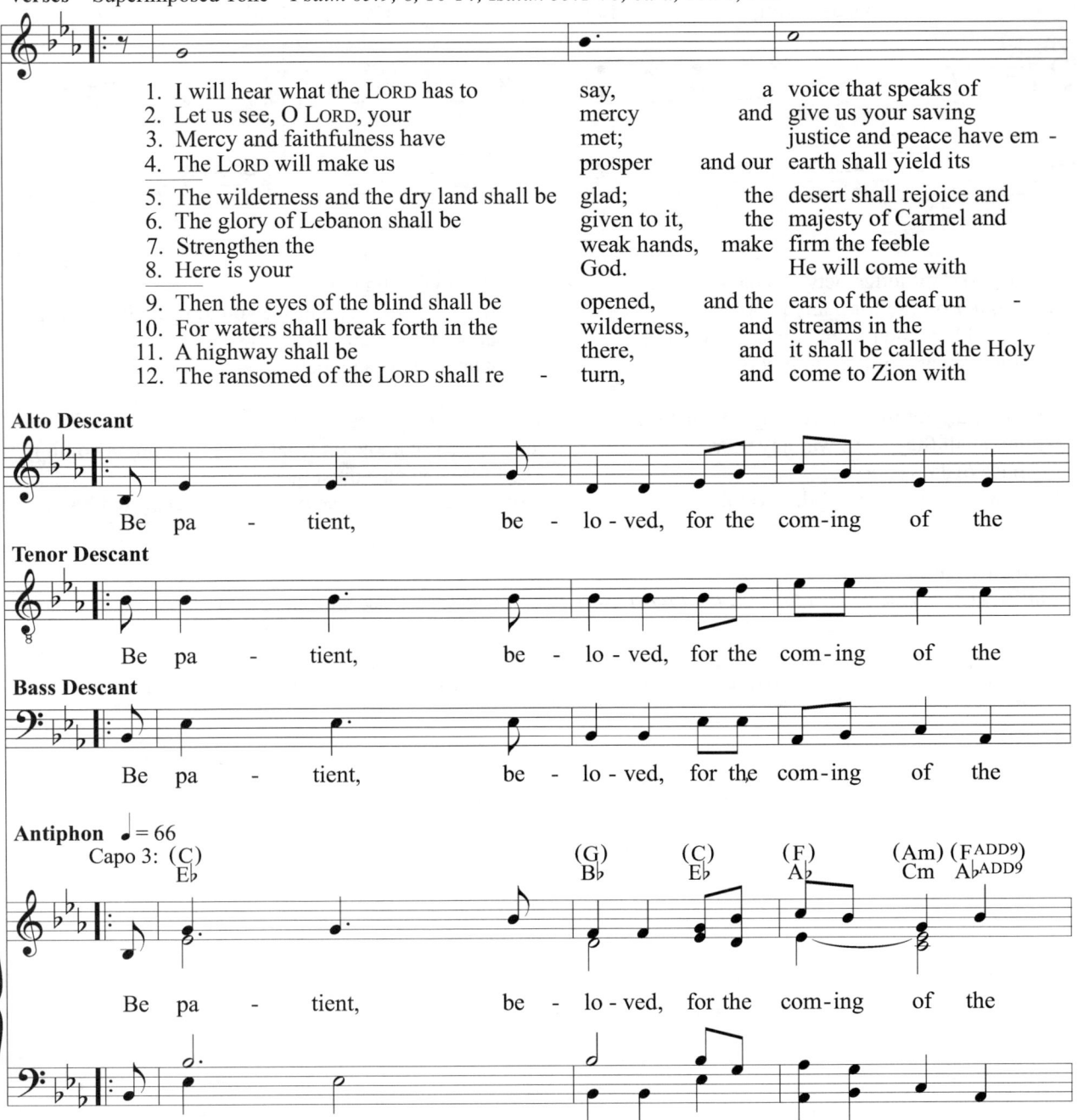

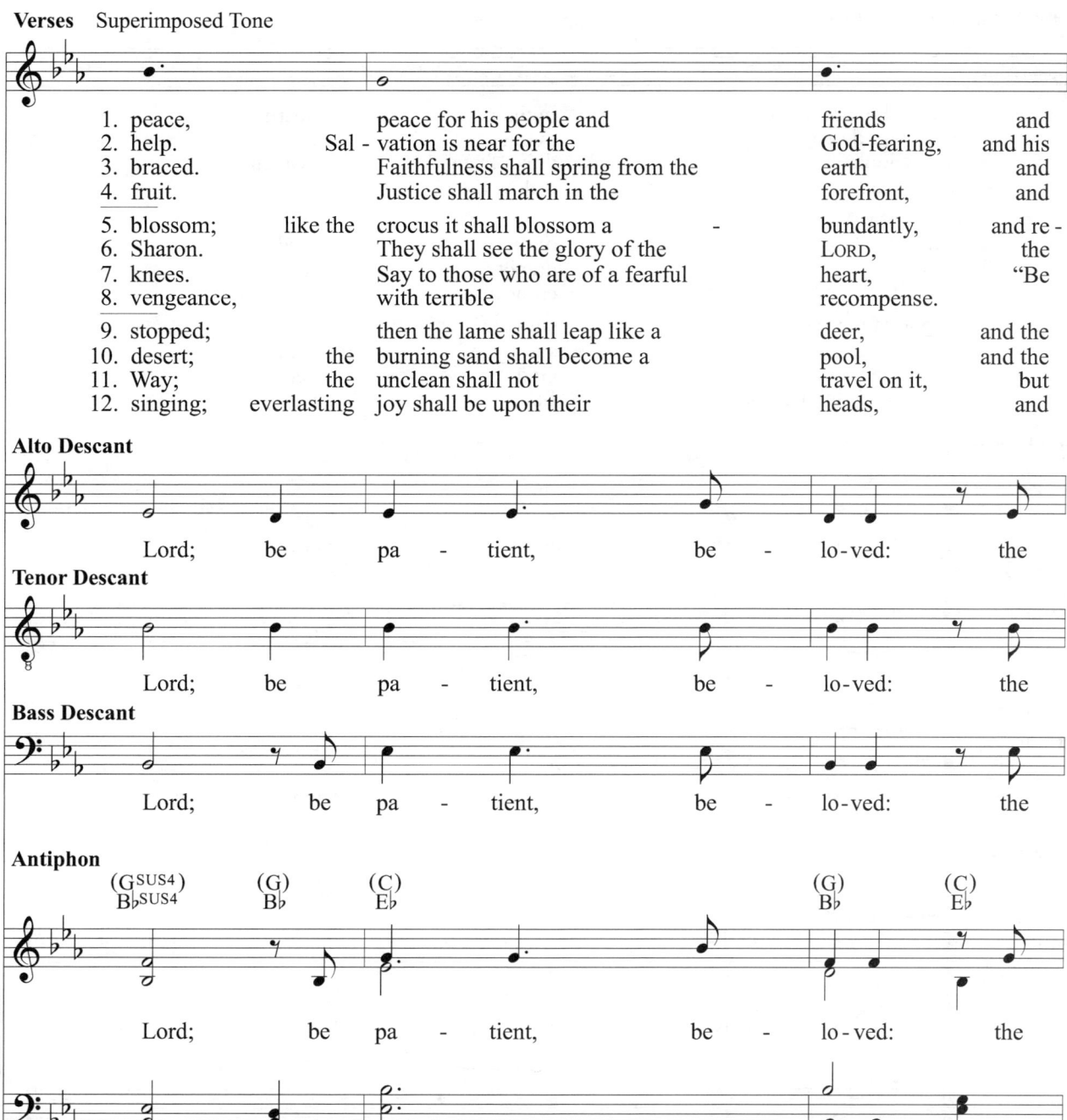

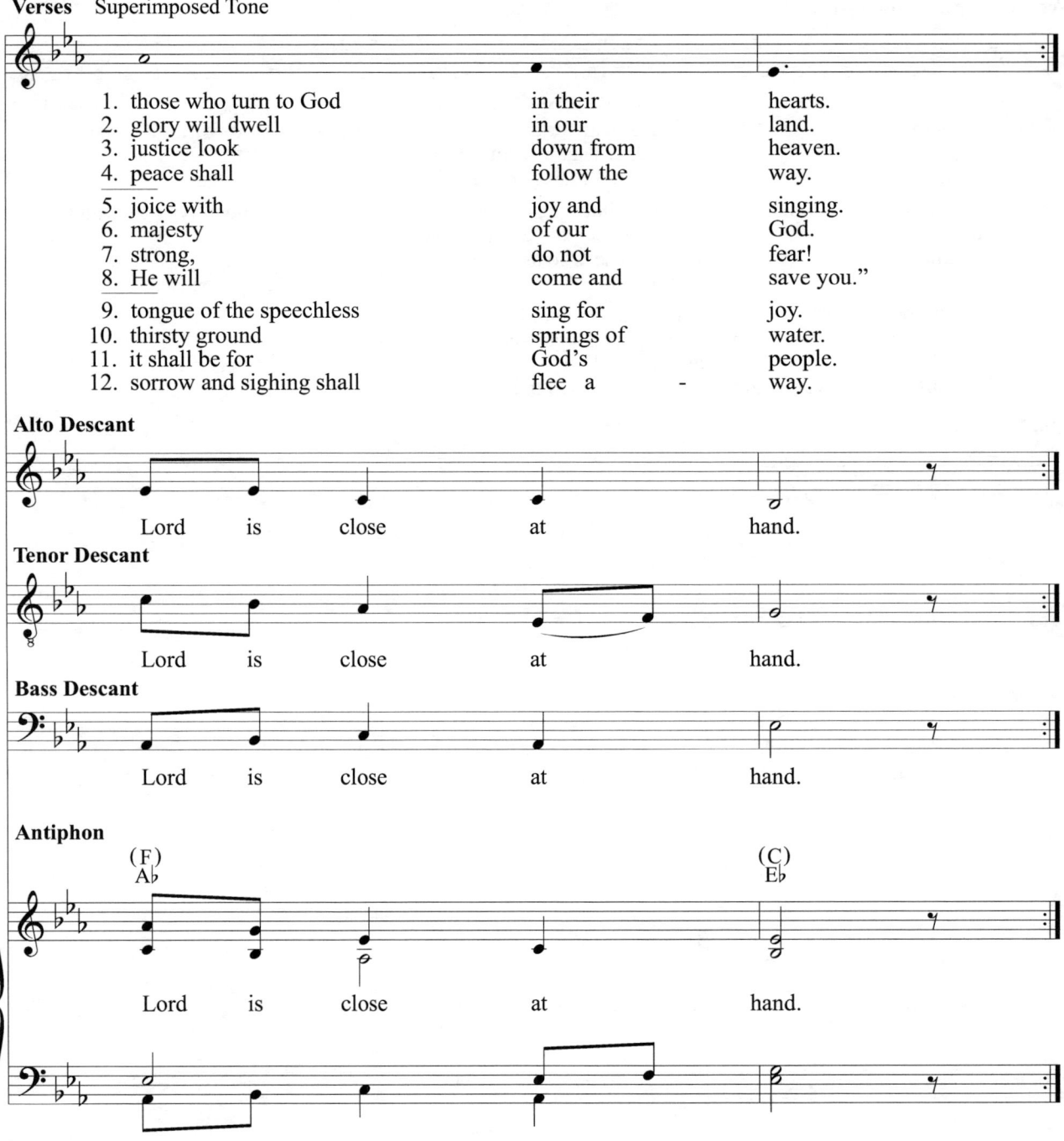

Let the King of Glory Come In

Fourth Sunday of Advent, Year A: Song for the Word

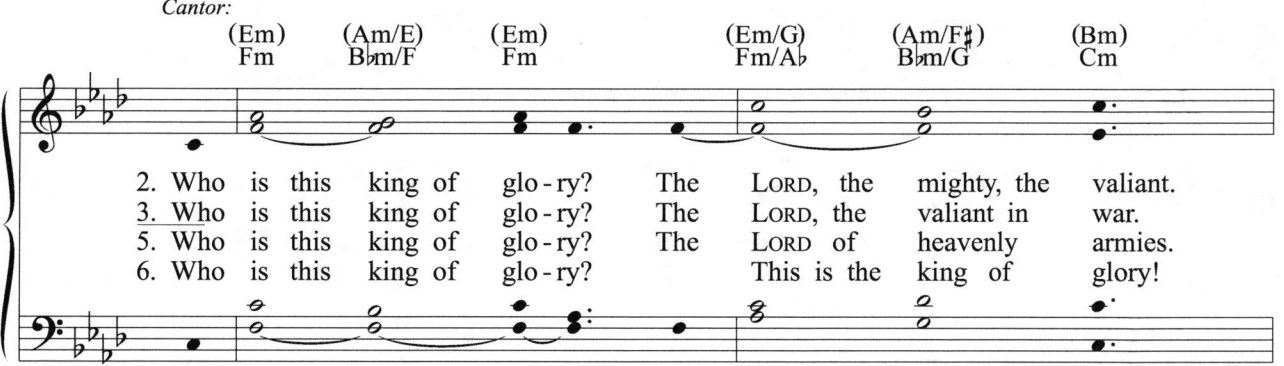
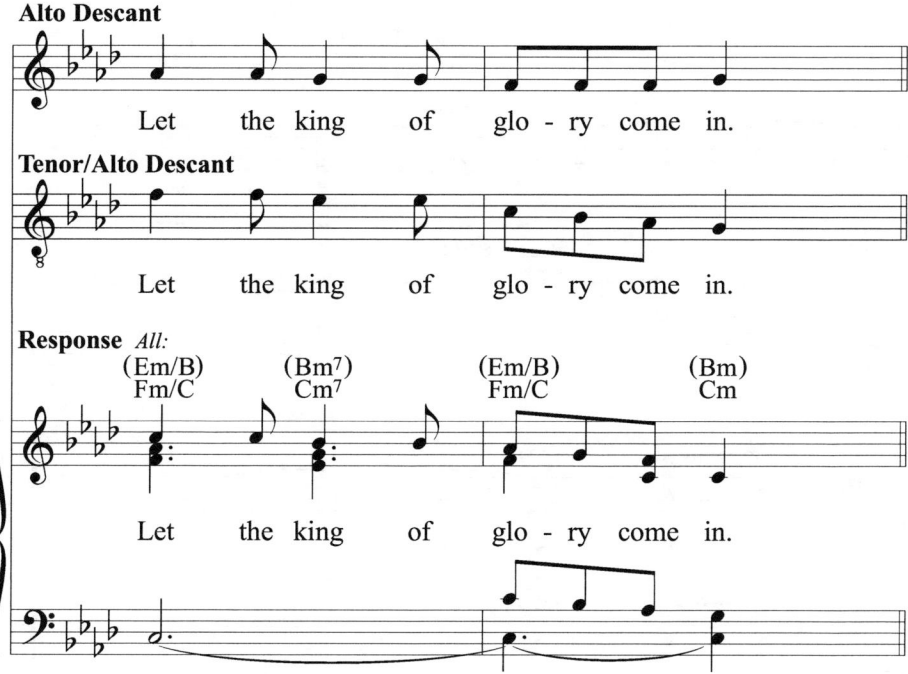

Psalm text: The Grail (England), © 1963, 1986, 1993, 2000, The Grail, GIA Publications, Inc., agent. All rights reserved. Used with permission.
Music and antiphon text: © 2005, The Collegeville Composers Group. All rights reserved. Published and administered by the Liturgical Press, Collegeville, MN 56321.

Jesus, Mighty Lord, Come Save Us

Fourth Sunday of Advent, Year A: Song for the Table

Verse Tone

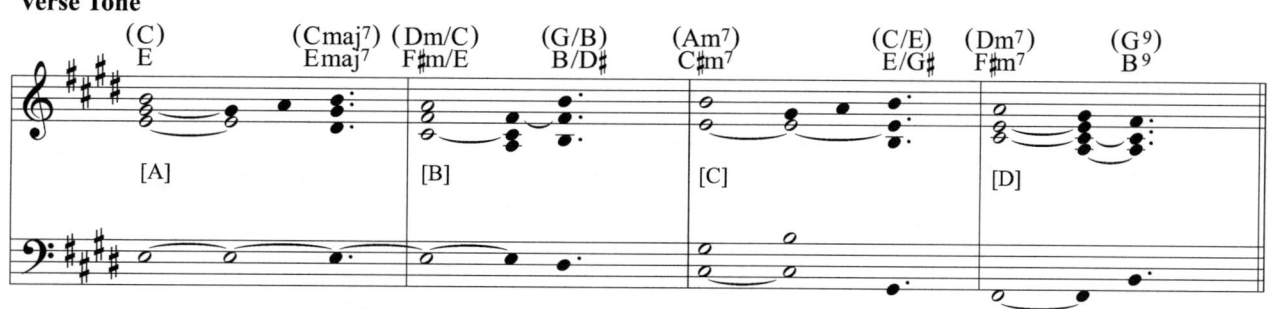

Psalm 19

1. The heavens proclaim the glo<u>ry</u> of God,
   and the firmament shows forth the work of <u>God's</u> hands.
   Day unto day takes <u>up</u> the story
   and night unto night makes known <u>the</u> message.

2. No speech, no word, no <u>voice</u> is heard
   yet their span extends through all <u>the</u> earth,
   [Omit C]
   their words to the utmost bounds of <u>the</u> world.

3. There God has placed a tent <u>for</u> the sun;
   it comes forth like a bridegroom coming from <u>his</u> tent,
   [Omit C]
   rejoices like a champion to run <u>its</u> course.

4. At the end of the sky is the rising <u>of</u> the sun;
   to the furthest end of the sky is <u>its</u> course.
   [Omit C]
   There is nothing concealed from its burn<u>ing</u> heat.

5. The law of the L<small>ORD</small> is perfect,
   it revives <u>the</u> soul.
   The rule of the L<small>ORD</small> is <u>to</u> be trusted,
   it gives wisdom to <u>the</u> simple.

6. The precepts of the L<small>ORD</small> are right,
   they gladden <u>the</u> heart.

The command of the L<small>ORD</small> is clear,
it gives light to <u>the</u> eyes.

7. The fear of the L<small>ORD</small> is holy,
   abiding <u>for</u> ever.
   The decrees of the L<small>ORD</small> are truth
   and all of <u>them</u> just.

8. They are more to be de<u>sired</u> than gold,
   than the purest <u>of</u> gold
   and sweeter are <u>they</u> than honey,
   than honey from <u>the</u> comb.

9. So in them your servant <u>finds</u> instruction;
   great reward is in <u>their</u> keeping.
   But can we discern <u>all</u> our errors?
   From hidden faults <u>acquit</u> us.

10. From presumption re<u>strain</u> your servant
    and let it <u>not</u> rule me.
    Then shall <u>I</u> be blameless,
    clean from <u>grave</u> sin.

11. May the spoken words <u>of</u> my mouth,
    the thoughts of <u>my</u> heart,
    win favor in your <u>sight</u>, O L<small>ORD</small>,
    my rescuer, <u>my</u> rock!

Performance Notes

The Antiphon may be sung in unison, or as a round as indicated.

It is recommended that guitars are not used to accompany the Antiphon when sung as a round, since the chord-changes would be too rapid. For the purposes of giving the pitch only, the asterisked chord in square brackets at the beginning of the Antiphon may be used. Guitar chords are provided for the Verse Tone as usual.

The melody of the Antiphon is derived from the hymn tune Divinum Mysterium *("Of the Father's love begotten").*

Psalm text: The Grail (England), © 1963, 1986, 1993, 2000, The Grail, GIA Publications, Inc., agent. All rights reserved. Used with permission.
Music and antiphon text: © 2007, The Collegeville Composers Group. All rights reserved. Published and administered by the Liturgical Press, Collegeville, MN 56321.

Clothed in Christ, One in Christ

Baptism of the Lord, Year A: Song for the Table
Easter Vigil: Baptismal Acclamation

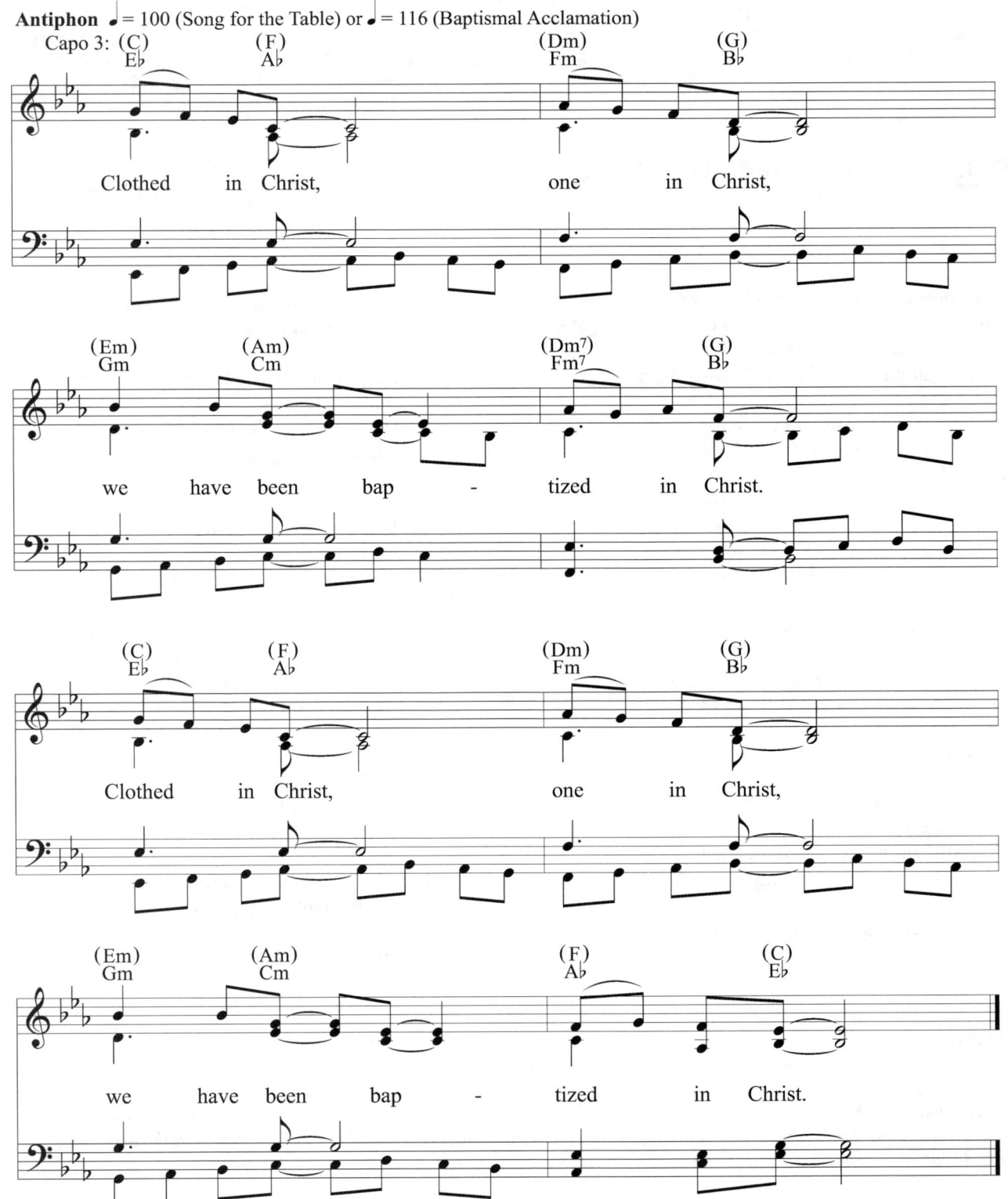

Performance Notes
During the Rite of Baptism, the antiphon may be used as an acclamation immediately after each baptism, or at the clothing with a white garment, or at both moments in the Rite.

Verse Tone

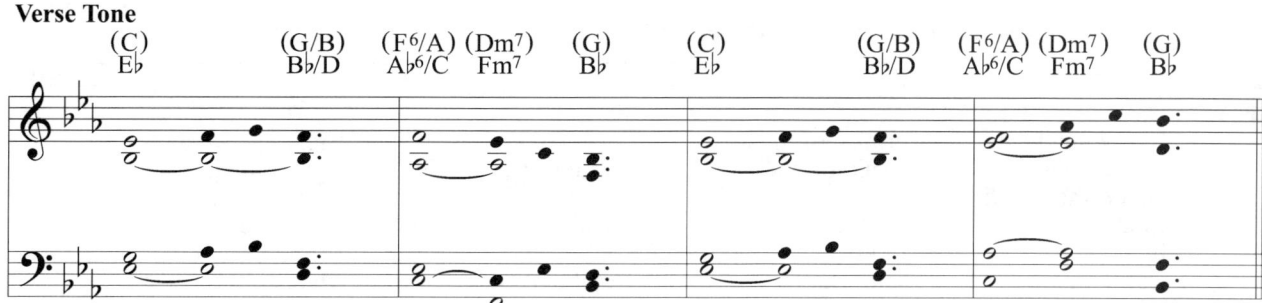

Titus 3:4-7; Ephesians 1:3-12; 1 Timothy 3:16

1. When the goodness and loving kindness of God our Sa<u>vior</u> appeared,
   he saved us, not because of any works of righteousness that <u>we</u> had done,
   but according <u>to</u> his mercy,
   through the water of rebirth and renewal by the <u>Ho</u>ly Spirit.

2. This Spirit he poured out on us richly through Jesus <u>Christ</u> our Savior,
   so that, having been justified <u>by</u> his grace,
   we might <u>be</u>come heirs
   according to the hope of e<u>ter</u>nal life.

3. Blessed be the God and Father of our Lord <u>Je</u>sus Christ,
   who has blessed us in Christ with every spiritual blessing in the <u>heaven</u>ly places,
   just as he chose us in Christ before the foundation <u>of</u> the world
   to be holy and blameless before <u>him</u> in love.

4. He destined us for adoption as his children through <u>Je</u>sus Christ,
   according to the good pleasure <u>of</u> his will,
   to the praise of his <u>glo</u>rious grace
   that he freely bestowed on us in <u>the</u> Beloved.

5. In him we have redemption <u>through</u> his blood,
   the forgiveness <u>of</u> our trespasses,
   according to the riches <u>of</u> his grace
   that he la<u>vished</u> on us.

6. With all wisdom and insight he has made known to us the mystery <u>of</u> his will,
   according to his good pleasure that he set <u>forth</u> in Christ,
   as a plan for the full<u>ness</u> of time,
   to gather up all things in him, things in heaven and <u>things</u> on earth.

7. In Christ we have also obtained <u>an</u> inheritance,
   having been destined according to the purpose of him who accomplishes all things
      according to his <u>coun</u>sel and will,
   so that we, who were the first to set our <u>hope</u> on Christ,
   might live for the praise <u>of</u> his glory.

8. He was revealed in flesh, vindi<u>cat</u>ed in spirit,
   seen by angels, proclaimed <u>among</u> Gentiles,
   believed in through<u>out</u> the world,
   taken <u>up</u> in glory.

Canticle text: NRSV Bible, © 1989, Division of Christian Education of the National Council of the Churches of Christ in the United States of America. All rights reserved.
Music and antiphon text: © 2005, The Collegeville Composers Group. All rights reserved. Published and administered by the Liturgical Press, Collegeville, MN 56321.

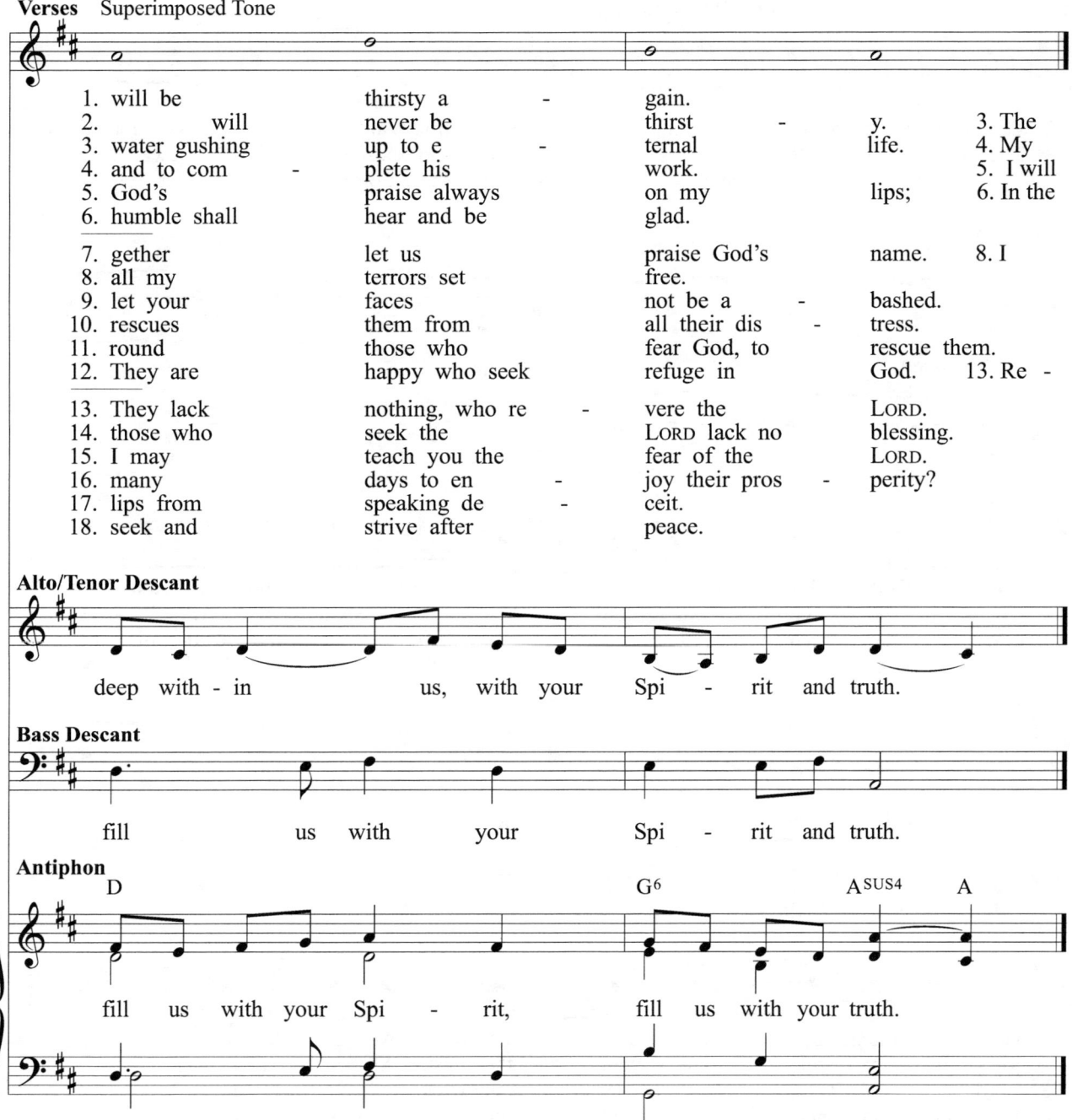

Give Thanks to the Lord, Alleluia

Second Sunday of Easter, Year A: Song for the Word

Music and text: © 2005, 2007, The Collegeville Composers Group. All rights reserved. Published and administered by the Liturgical Press, Collegeville, MN 56321.

At Your Word Our Hearts Are Burning
Third Sunday of Easter, Year A: Song for the Table

21

Revelation 4:11; 5:9-10, 12b-d, 13b-d; 4:8c

1. You are worthy, our Lord <u>and</u> God,
   to receive glory and h<u>on</u>or and power,
   for you cre<u>at</u>ed all things,
   and by your will <u>they</u> existed
   and <u>were</u> created.

2. You are worthy to take <u>the</u> scroll
   and to <u>op</u>en its seals,
   for you were slaughtered and by <u>your</u> blood
   you r<u>an</u>somed for God
   saints from every tribe and language and
       <u>peo</u>ple and nation;

3. *C* you have made them to be a kingdom <u>and</u> priests
   D ser<u>ving</u> our God,
   E and they will <u>reign</u> on earth.

4. *C* Worthy is the Lamb that <u>was</u> slaughtered
   D to receive power and wealth and wis<u>dom</u> and might
   E and honor and glo<u>ry</u> and blessing.

5. *C* To the one seated on the throne and to <u>the</u> Lamb
   D be blessing and honor and glo<u>ry</u> and might
   E fore<u>ver</u> and ever.

6. *C* Holy, hol<u>y</u>, holy,
   D the Lord God <u>the</u> Almighty,
   E who was and is and <u>is</u> to come.

Performance Notes

The Antiphon is the hymn tune STUTTGART. It would perhaps be preferable to perform this in chant style, unaccompanied, at half-note = ca. 80.

Canticle text: NRSV Bible, © 1989, Division of Christian Education of the National Council of the Churches of Christ in the United States of America. All rights reserved.
Antiphon melody: STUTTGART, 87 87, Christian Friedrich Witt, 1660–1716. Arrangement, verse tone and antiphon text: © 2007, The Collegeville Composers Group. All rights reserved.
Published and administered by the Liturgical Press, Collegeville, MN 56321.

I Am the Way: Follow Me
Fifth Sunday of Easter, Year A: Song for the Table

I Am the Way: Follow Me, pg. 2

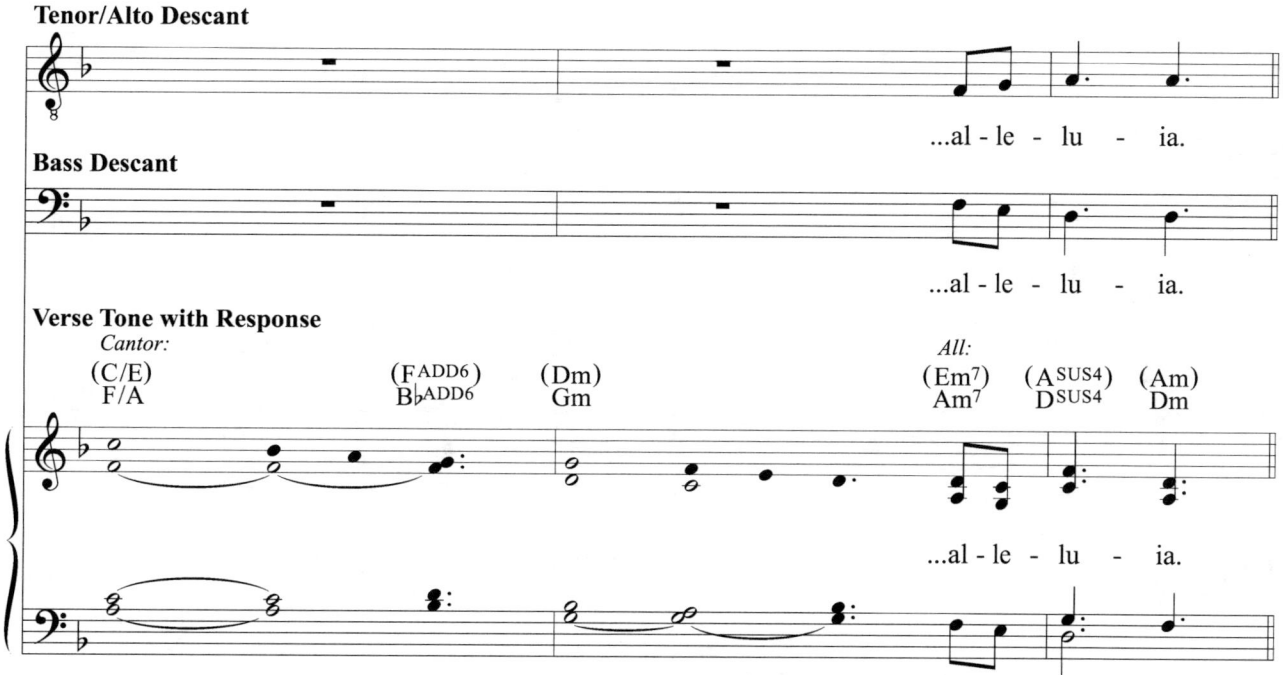

Cf. John 15:5; 10:11; 14:27; Revelation 19:5; 12:10; Romans 6:8; Psalm 71:8, 23a; 2 Corinthians 5:15; Revelation 5:12; Colossians 2:12; John 17:20-21

1. I am the vine and you are the branches,
   <u>says</u> the Lord;
   those who abide in me, and I in them, <u>bear</u> much fruit, *alleluia.*

2. The Good Shepherd is risen, who laid down his life <u>for</u> his sheep,
   the one is risen who died <u>for</u> his flock, *alleluia.*

3. Peace I leave with you, my peace I give to you,
   <u>says</u> the Lord.
   Not as the world gives <u>do</u> I give to you, *alleluia.*

4. Praise our God, all <u>you</u> his servants,
   and all who fear him, <u>small</u> and great, *alleluia.*

5. Now have come the salvation <u>and</u> the power
   and the kingdom of our God
   and the authority of <u>his</u> Anointed, *alleluia.*

6. If we have <u>died</u> with Christ,
   we believe that we will also <u>live</u> with him, *alleluia.*

7. Our lips are filled with your praise <u>and</u> your glory;
   when we sing to you our lips <u>shall</u> rejoice, *alleluia.*

8. Christ has risen and <u>shines</u> upon us;
   he has redeemed us <u>with</u> his blood, *alleluia.*

9. Christ died for all, so that those who live might live no longer <u>for</u> themselves,
   but for him who died <u>and</u> was raised for them, *alleluia.*

10. Worthy is the Lamb <u>that</u> was slain
    to receive power and wealth and wisdom and might and honor and <u>glory</u> and blessing, *alleluia.*

11. The one who died on the cross has risen <u>from</u> the dead,
    and has rescued our <u>lives</u> from death, *alleluia.*

12. When we were buried with Christ in baptism,
    we were <u>also</u> raised with him
    through faith in the power of God, who raised him <u>from</u> the dead, *alleluia.*

13. I pray for them, Father, that they may be one in us, <u>says</u> the Lord,
    so that the world may believe that <u>you</u> have sent me, *alleluia.*

Part canticle text: NRSV Bible, © 1989, Division of Christian Education of the National Council of the Churches of Christ in the United States of America. All rights reserved.
Psalm text: The Grail (England), © 1963, 1986, 1993, 2000, The Grail, GIA Publications, Inc., agent. All rights reserved. Used with permission.
Music and antiphon / part canticle texts: © 2007, The Collegeville Composers Group. All rights reserved. Published and administered by the Liturgical Press, Collegeville, MN 56321.

Here I Am
Second Sunday in Ordinary Time, Year A: Song for the Word

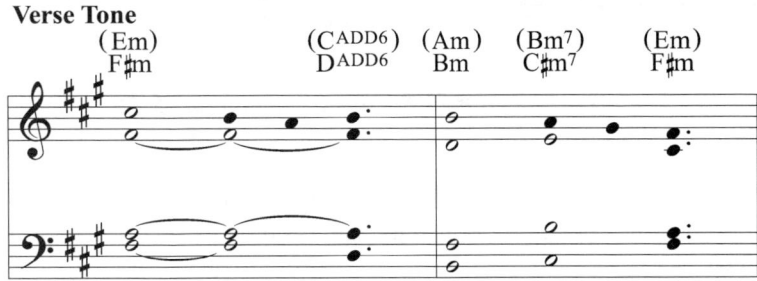

Psalm 40:2, 4ab, 7-11

1. I waited, I waited <u>for</u> the Lord
   who stooped down to me, and <u>heard</u> my cry.

2. God put a new song in<u>to</u> my mouth,
   praise <u>of</u> our God.

3. You do not ask for sacri<u>fice</u> and offerings,
   but an <u>open</u> ear.

4. You do not ask for holo<u>caust</u> and victim.
   Instead, <u>here</u> am I.

5. In the scroll of the book <u>it</u> stands written
   that I should <u>do</u> your will.

6. My God, I delight <u>in</u> your law
   in the depth <u>of</u> my heart.

7. Your justice I <u>have</u> proclaimed
   in the <u>great</u> assembly.

8. My lips I <u>have</u> not sealed;
   you know <u>it</u>, O Lord.

9. I have not hidden your justice <u>in</u> my heart
   but declared your <u>faithful</u> help.

10. I have not hidden your love <u>and</u> your truth
    from the <u>great</u> assembly.

Performance Notes
The Antiphon may be sung twice each time if desired.
The descants are intended for equal voices.

Psalm text: The Grail (England), © 1963, 1986, 1993, 2000, The Grail, GIA Publications, Inc., agent. All rights reserved. Used with permission.
Music and antiphon text: © 2005, The Collegeville Composers Group. All rights reserved. Published and administered by the Liturgical Press, Collegeville, MN 56321.

Light of the World
Third Sunday in Ordinary Time, Year A: Song for the Table

Light of the World, pg. 3

In God Alone Is My Soul at Rest
Eighth Sunday in Ordinary Time, Year A: Song for the Word

Psalm 62:2-3, 6-9c

1. In God alone is my soul at rest;
   in God alone
   from God comes my help.

2. God alone is my rock, my stronghold,
   in God alone
   my fortress; I stand firm.

3. In God alone be at rest, my soul;
   in God alone
   from God comes my hope.

4. God alone is my rock, my stronghold,
   in God alone
   my fortress; I stand firm.

5. In God is my safety and glory,
   in God alone
   the rock of my strength.

6. Take refuge in God, all you people;
   in God alone
   trusting always, pour out your hearts to the Lord.

Psalm text: The Grail (England), © 1963, 1986, 1993, 2000, The Grail, GIA Publications, Inc., agent. All rights reserved. Used with permission.
Music and antiphon text: © 2007, The Collegeville Composers Group. All rights reserved. Published and administered by the Liturgical Press, Collegeville, MN 56321.

Keep These Words in Your Heart and Soul
Ninth Sunday in Ordinary Time, Year A: Song for the Table

Psalm 17:1-9, 15

1. LORD, hear a <u>cause</u> that is <u>just</u>,
   pay heed to <u>my</u> cry.
   Turn your <u>ear</u> to my <u>prayer</u>,
   no deceit <u>is</u> on my lips.

2. From you may my <u>judgement</u> come <u>forth</u>.
   Your eyes discern <u>the</u> truth.
   You search my heart, you <u>visit</u> me by <u>night</u>.
   You test me and you find <u>in</u> me no wrong.

3. My words are not <u>sinful</u> like human <u>words</u>.
   I kept from violence because of <u>your</u> word,
   I kept my feet <u>firmly</u> in your <u>paths</u>;
   there was no faltering in my steps.

4. I am here and I call, you will <u>hear</u> me, O God.
   Turn your ear to me; hear <u>my</u> words.
   Display your great love, you whose <u>right</u> hand <u>saves</u>
   your friends from those who <u>rebel</u> against them.

5. Guard me as the <u>apple</u> of your <u>eye</u>.
   Hide me in the shadow of <u>your</u> wings
   from the violent <u>attack</u> of the <u>wicked</u>.
   My foes encircle me <u>with</u> <u>deadly</u> intent.

6. As for <u>me</u>, in my <u>justice</u>,
   I shall see <u>your</u> face
   and be <u>filled</u>, when I a<u>wake</u>,
   with <u>the</u> <u>sight of</u> your glory.

Performance Notes
In verses 5 and 6, line 4, the double underlined text is sung on a single note.

Psalm text: The Grail (England), © 1963, 1986, 1993, 2000, The Grail, GIA Publications, Inc., agent. All rights reserved. Used with permission.
Music and antiphon text: © 2007, The Collegeville Composers Group. All rights reserved. Published and administered by the Liturgical Press, Collegeville, MN 56321.

Love Is My Desire

Tenth Sunday in Ordinary Time, Year A: Song for the Table

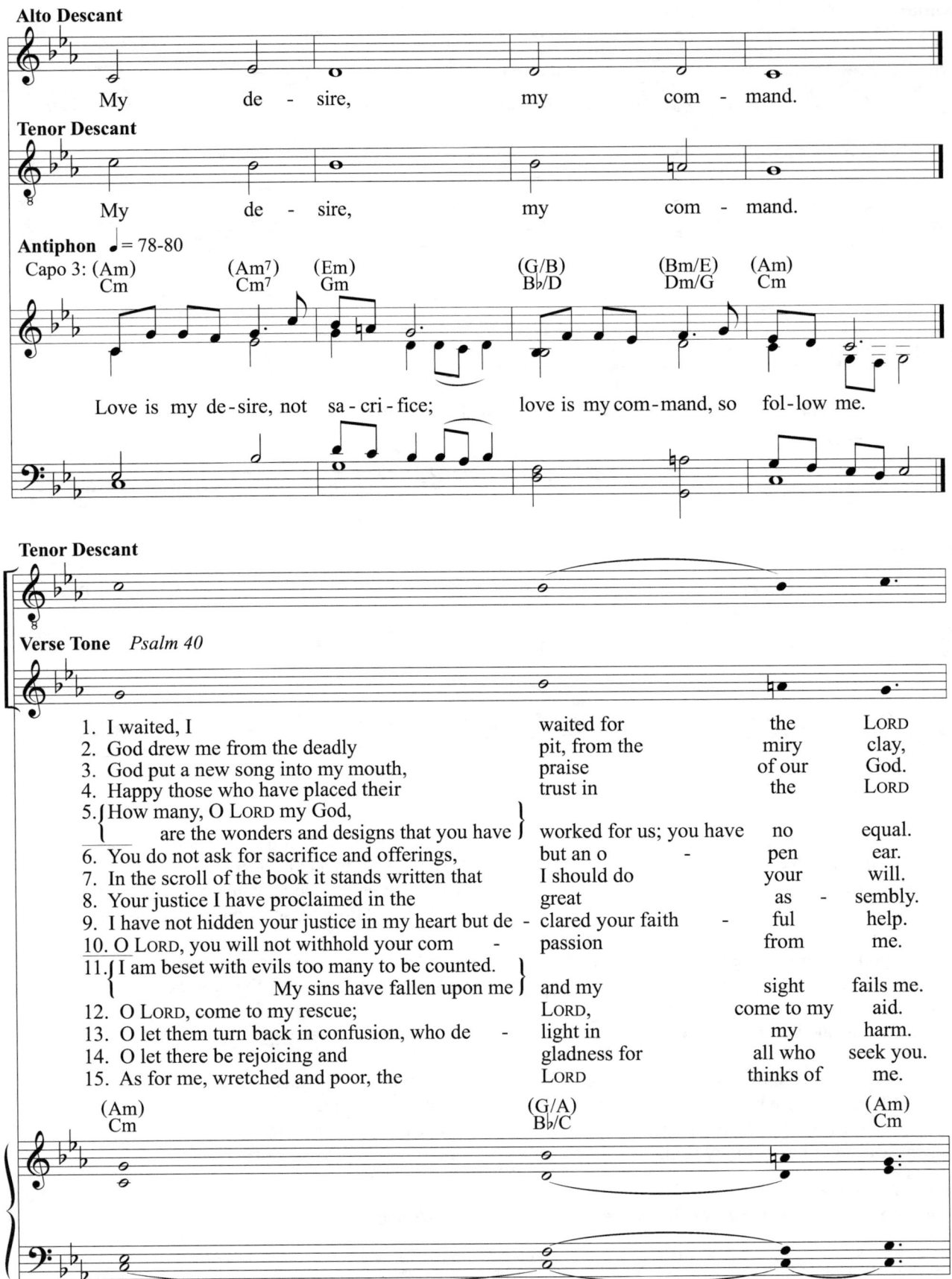

Love Is My Desire, pg. 2

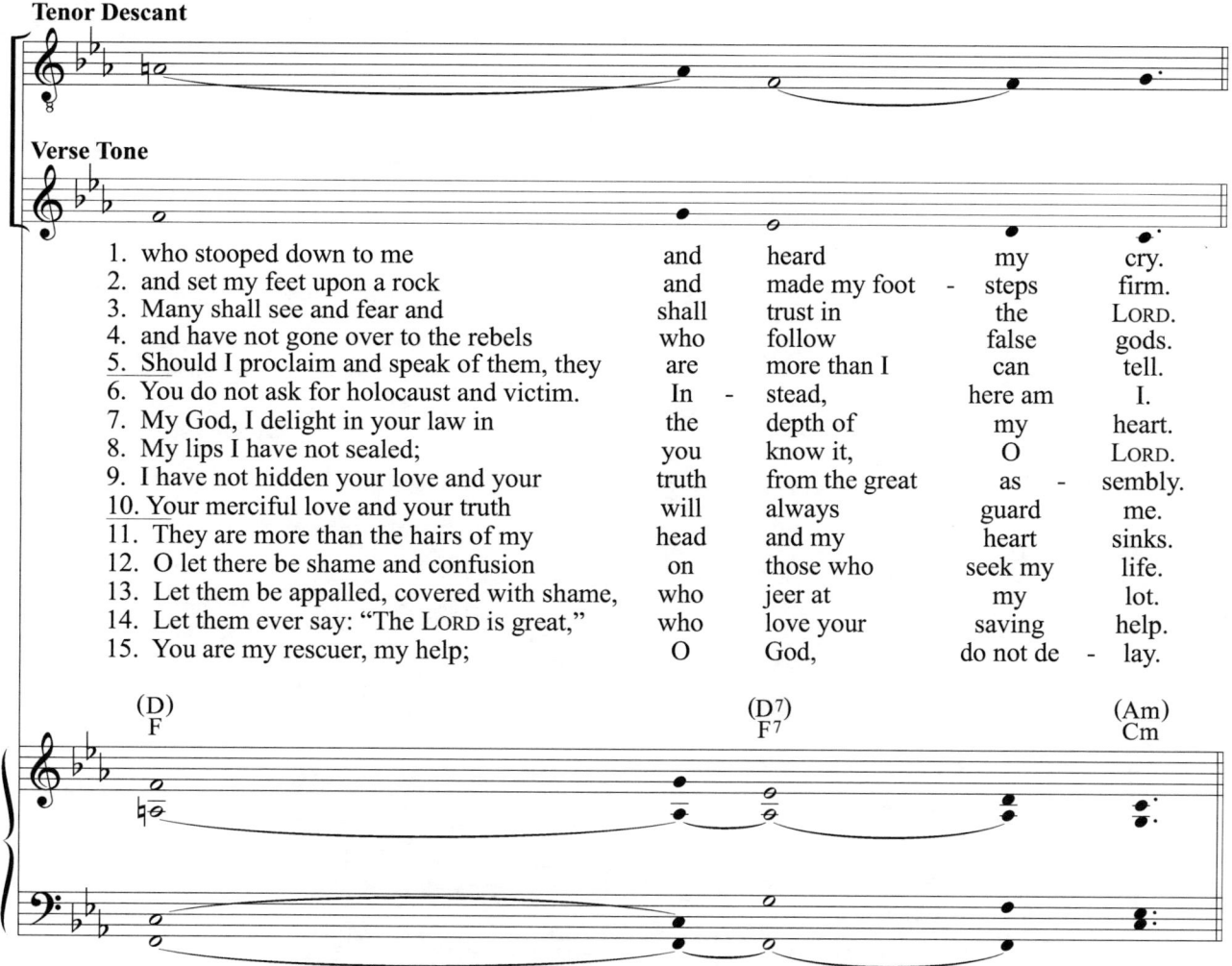

1. who stooped down to me and heard my cry.
2. and set my feet upon a rock and made my foot - steps firm.
3. Many shall see and fear and shall trust in the Lord.
4. and have not gone over to the rebels who follow false gods.
5. Should I proclaim and speak of them, they are more than I can tell.
6. You do not ask for holocaust and victim. In - stead, here am I.
7. My God, I delight in your law in the depth of my heart.
8. My lips I have not sealed; you know it, O Lord.
9. I have not hidden your love and your truth from the great as - sembly.
10. Your merciful love and your truth will always guard me.
11. They are more than the hairs of my head and my heart sinks.
12. O let there be shame and confusion on those who seek my life.
13. Let them be appalled, covered with shame, who jeer at my lot.
14. Let them ever say: "The Lord is great," who love your saving help.
15. You are my rescuer, my help; O God, do not de - lay.

Psalm text: The Grail (England), © 1963, 1986, 1993, 2000, The Grail, GIA Publications, Inc., agent. All rights reserved. Used with permission.
Music and antiphon text: © 2007, The Collegeville Composers Group. All rights reserved. Published and administered by the Liturgical Press, Collegeville, MN 56321.

The Mercy of God Is for All

Twentieth Sunday in Ordinary Time, Year A: Song for the Table

33

Verse Tone with Response *Psalm 130:1-6b, 7b-8; 103:1-4, 8, 10-14, 17-18*

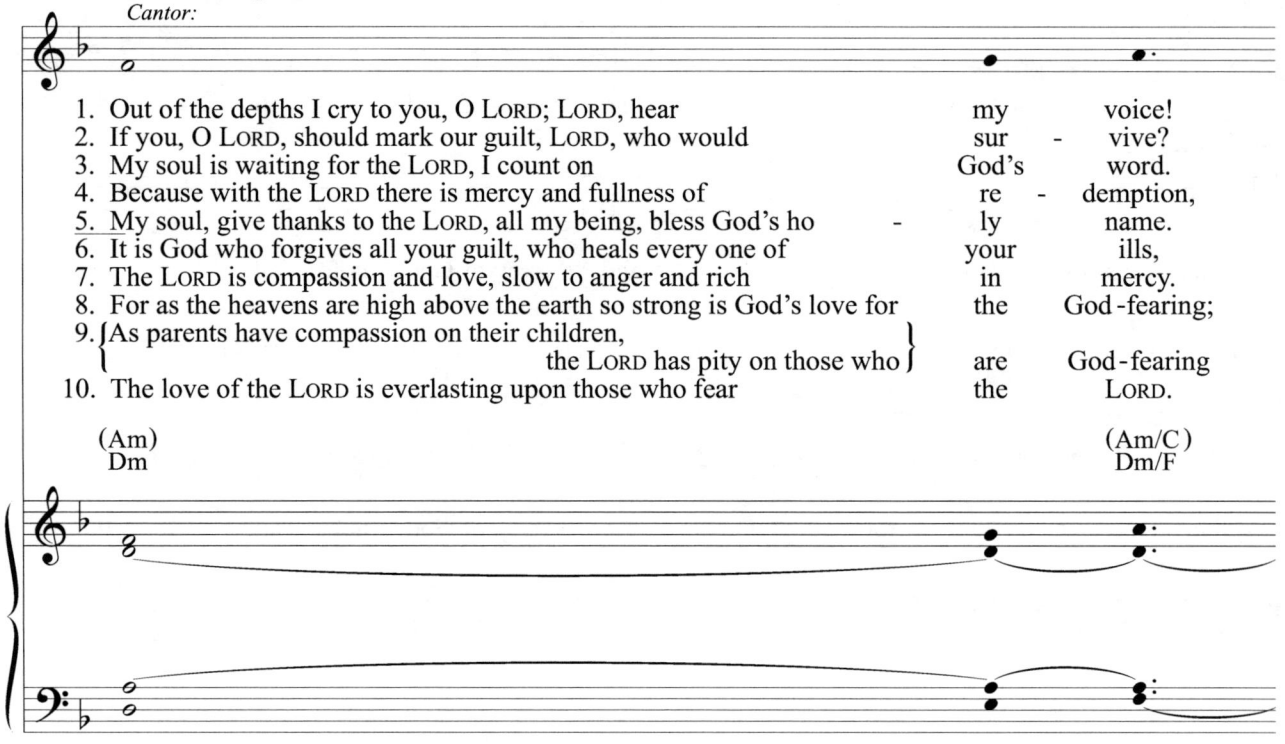

1. Out of the depths I cry to you, O Lord; Lord, hear my voice!
2. If you, O Lord, should mark our guilt, Lord, who would sur - vive?
3. My soul is waiting for the Lord, I count on God's word.
4. Because with the Lord there is mercy and fullness of re - demption,
5. My soul, give thanks to the Lord, all my being, bless God's ho - ly name.
6. It is God who forgives all your guilt, who heals every one of your ills,
7. The Lord is compassion and love, slow to anger and rich in mercy.
8. For as the heavens are high above the earth so strong is God's love for the God-fearing;
9. {As parents have compassion on their children, the Lord has pity on those who} are God-fearing
10. The love of the Lord is everlasting upon those who fear the Lord.

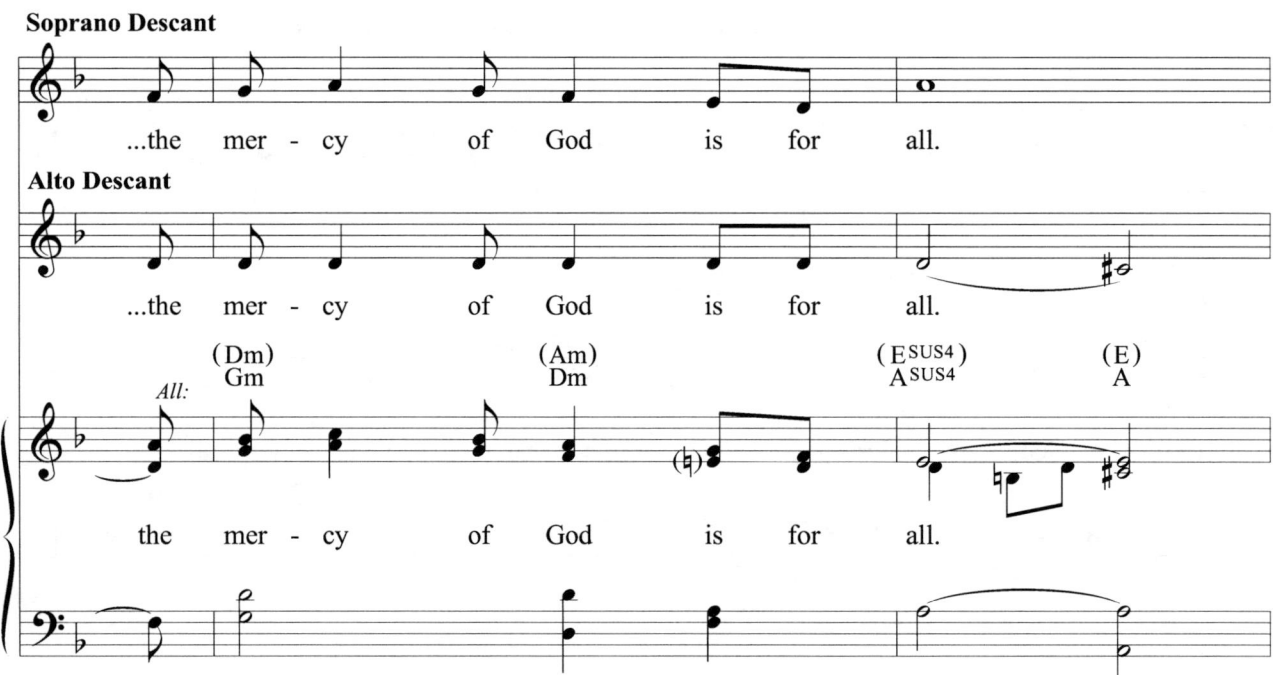

The Mercy of God Is for All, pg. 3

Verse Tone with Response

1. O let your ears be attentive to the voice of my pleading;
2. But with you is found forgiveness: for this we re - vere you.
3. My soul is longing for the LORD more than those who watch for daybreak.
4. Israel indeed God will redeem from all its in - iquity.
5. My soul, give thanks to the LORD and never forget all God's blessings.
6. who redeems your life from the grave, who crowns you with love and com - passion.
7. God does not treat us according to our sins nor repay us according to our faults.
8. As far as the east is from the west so far does he re - move our sins.
9. for he knows of what we are made, and remembers that we are dust.
10. God's justice reaches out to children's children when they keep his covenant in truth, when they keep his will in their mind.

Soprano Descant

Alto Descant

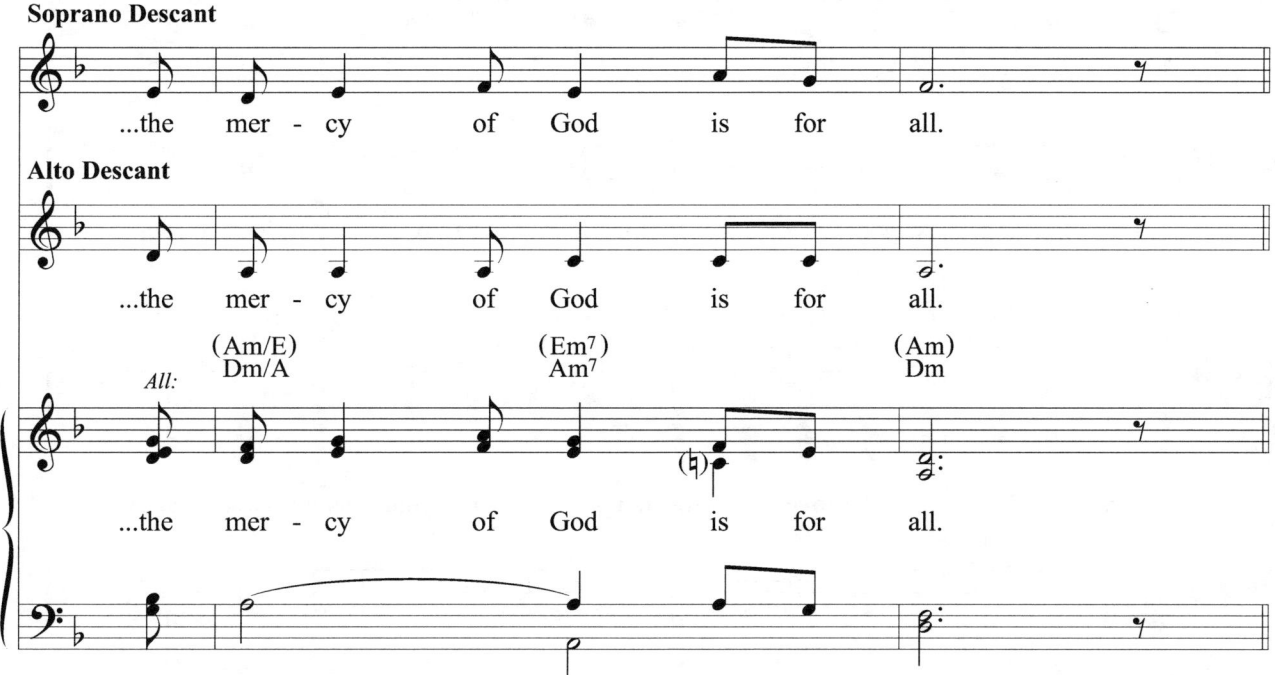

...the mer - cy of God is for all.

Psalm text: The Grail (England), © 1963, 1986, 1993, 2000, The Grail, GIA Publications, Inc., agent. All rights reserved. Used with permission.
Music and antiphon text: © 2007, The Collegeville Composers Group. All rights reserved. Published and administered by the Liturgical Press, Collegeville, MN 56321.

Everlasting Is Your Love
Twenty-first Sunday in Ordinary Time, Year A: Song for the Word

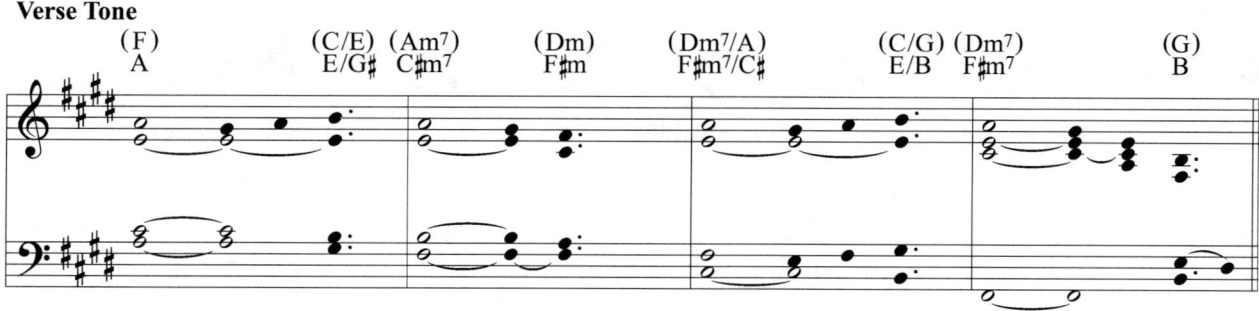

Psalm 138:1-3, 6, 8bc

1. I thank you, LORD, with <u>all</u> my heart,
   you have heard the words of <u>my</u> mouth.
   In the presence of the angels <u>I</u> will bless you.
   I will adore before your <u>ho</u>ly temple.

2. I thank you for your faithful<u>ness</u> and love
   which excel all we <u>ever</u> knew of you.
   On the day I <u>called</u>, you answered;
   you increased the strength <u>of</u> my soul.

3. The LORD is high yet looks <u>on</u> the lowly
   and the haughty God knows from <u>a</u>far.
   Your love, O LORD, <u>is</u> eternal,
   discard not the work <u>of</u> your hands.

Psalm text: The Grail (England), © 1963, 1986, 1993, 2000, The Grail, GIA Publications, Inc., agent. All rights reserved. Used with permission.
Music and antiphon text: © 2007, The Collegeville Composers Group. All rights reserved. Published and administered by the Liturgical Press, Collegeville, MN 56321.

All Things Are from the Lord

Twenty-first Sunday in Ordinary Time, Year A: Song for the Table

Verse Tone

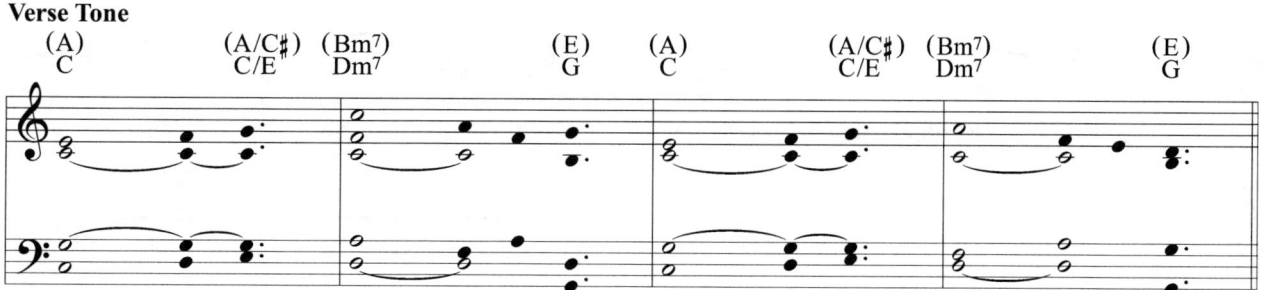

Psalm 104:1-2a, 13-15, 27-28, 29b-34

1. Bless the LORD, my soul!
   LORD God, how great you are,
   clothed in majesty and glory,
   wrapped in light as in a robe!

2. From your dwelling you water the hills;
   earth drinks its fill of your gift.
   You make the grass grow for the cattle
   and the plants to serve our needs.

3. May we bring forth bread from the earth
   and wine to cheer our hearts;
   oil to make our faces shine
   and bread to strengthen our hearts.

4. All things look to you
   to give them their food in due season.
   You give it, they gather it up;
   you open your hand, they have their fill.

5. You take back your spirit, they die,
   returning to the dust from which they came.
   You send forth your spirit, they are created;
   and you renew the face of the earth.

6. May the glory of the LORD last for ever!
   May the LORD rejoice in creation!
   God looks on the earth and it trembles;
   at God's touch, the mountains send forth smoke.

7. I will sing to the LORD all my life,
   make music to my God while I live.
   May my thoughts be pleasing to God.
   I find my joy in the LORD.

Psalm text: The Grail (England), © 1963, 1986, 1993, 2000, The Grail, GIA Publications, Inc., agent. All rights reserved. Used with permission.
Music and antiphon text: © 2007, The Collegeville Composers Group. All rights reserved. Published and administered by the Liturgical Press, Collegeville, MN 56321.

Where Two or Three Are Gathered

Twenty-third Sunday in Ordinary Time, Year A: Song for the Table

Verse Tone

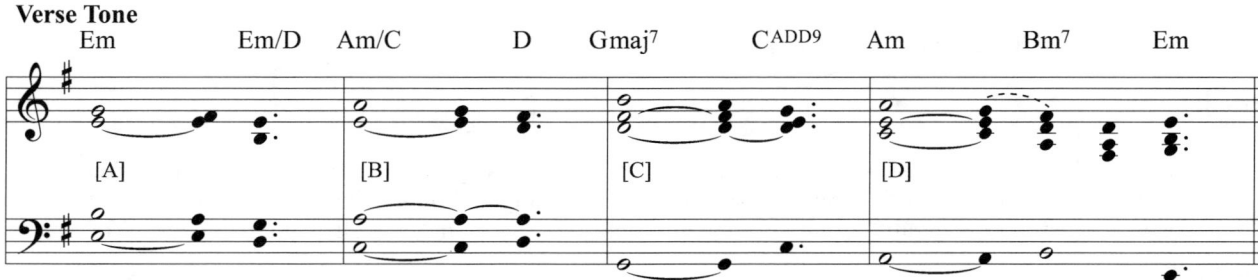

Romans 12:1-2, 4-5, 9-17, 20ab, 21; 13:8, 9a, 9g-10; 14:8-9; 15:5-7

1. I appeal to you, brothers <u>and</u> sisters,
   by the mercies <u>of</u> God,
   to present your bodies as a liv<u>ing</u> sacrifice,
   holy and accept<u>a</u>ble to God.

2. Do not be conformed to <u>this</u> world,
   but be transformed by the renewing of <u>your</u> minds,
   so that you may discern what is the will <u>of</u> God,
   what is good and accept<u>a</u>ble and perfect.

3. For as in one body we have ma<u>ny</u> members,
   and not all the members have the <u>same</u> function,
   so we, who are many, are one body <u>in</u> Christ,
   and individually we are members <u>of</u> one another.

4. Let love be genuine; hate what <u>is</u> evil,
   hold fast to what <u>is</u> good;
   love one another with mutual a<u>ffec</u>tion:
   outdo one another <u>in</u> showing honor.

5. Do not lag <u>in</u> zeal,
   be ardent in spirit, serve <u>the</u> Lord.
   Rejoice in hope, be patient <u>in</u> suffering,
   pers<u>e</u>vere in prayer.
   [Repeat C-D]
   Contribute to the needs of <u>the</u> saints;
   extend hospit<u>a</u>lity to strangers.

6. Bless those <u>who</u> persecute you;
   bless and do <u>not</u> curse them.
   Rejoice with those who <u>re</u>joice,
   weep <u>with</u> those who weep.

7. Live in harmony with one a<u>noth</u>er;
   do not <u>be</u> haughty,
   but associate with <u>the</u> lowly;
   do not claim to be wis<u>er</u> than you are.
   [Repeat C-D]
   Do not repay anyone evil <u>for</u> evil,
   but take thought for what is noble in <u>the</u> sight of all.

8. If your enemies are hun<u>gry</u>, feed them;
   if they are thirsty, give them something <u>to</u> drink.
   Do not be overcome <u>by</u> evil,
   but overcome <u>e</u>vil with good.

9. Owe no <u>one</u> anything,
   except to love one a<u>noth</u>er;
   for the one who loves <u>a</u>nother
   has <u>ful</u>filled the law.

10. The commandments are summed up
    in <u>this</u> word:
    "Love your neighbor as your<u>self</u>."
    Love does no wrong to <u>a</u> neighbor;
    therefore, love is the fulfil<u>ling</u> of the law.

11. If we live, we live to <u>the</u> Lord,
    and if we die, we die to <u>the</u> Lord;
    so then, whether we live or whether <u>we</u> die,
    we <u>are</u>   the Lord's.
    [Repeat C-D]
    To this end Christ died and lived a<u>gain</u>,
    so that he might be Lord of both
    the <u>dead</u> and the living.

12. May the God of steadfastness and
    en<u>cour</u>agement
    grant you to live in harmony with one
    <u>a</u>nother,
    in accordance with <u>Christ</u> Jesus,
    so that together with one voice you may
    glorify the God and Father of our
    <u>Lord</u> Jesus Christ.

13. *[Omit A-B]*
    Welcome one another, therefore, just as
    Christ <u>has</u> welcomed you,
    for the <u>glo</u>ry of God.

Canticle text: NRSV Bible, © 1989, Division of Christian Education of the National Council of the Churches of Christ in the United States of America. All rights reserved.
Music and antiphon text: © 2006, The Collegeville Composers Group. All rights reserved. Published and administered by the Liturgical Press, Collegeville, MN 56321.

Lord, You Are Close
Twenty-fifth Sunday in Ordinary Time, Year A: Song for the Word

Lord, You Are Close, pg. 2

Performance Notes
In measure 2, the cue-size notes in parentheses may be substituted if necessary.
The superimposed tone for a tenor cantor is intended as an alternative to the tenor descant - the two should not be sung concurrently.
The Antiphon melody is derived from the Gavotte in Bach's Suite #2 in B minor for flute and strings.

Psalm text: The Grail (England), © 1963, 1986, 1993, 2000, The Grail, GIA Publications, Inc., agent. All rights reserved. Used with permission.
Music and antiphon text: © 2007, The Collegeville Composers Group. All rights reserved. Published and administered by the Liturgical Press, Collegeville, MN 56321.

Remember, Lord

Twenty-sixth Sunday in Ordinary Time, Year A: Song for the Word

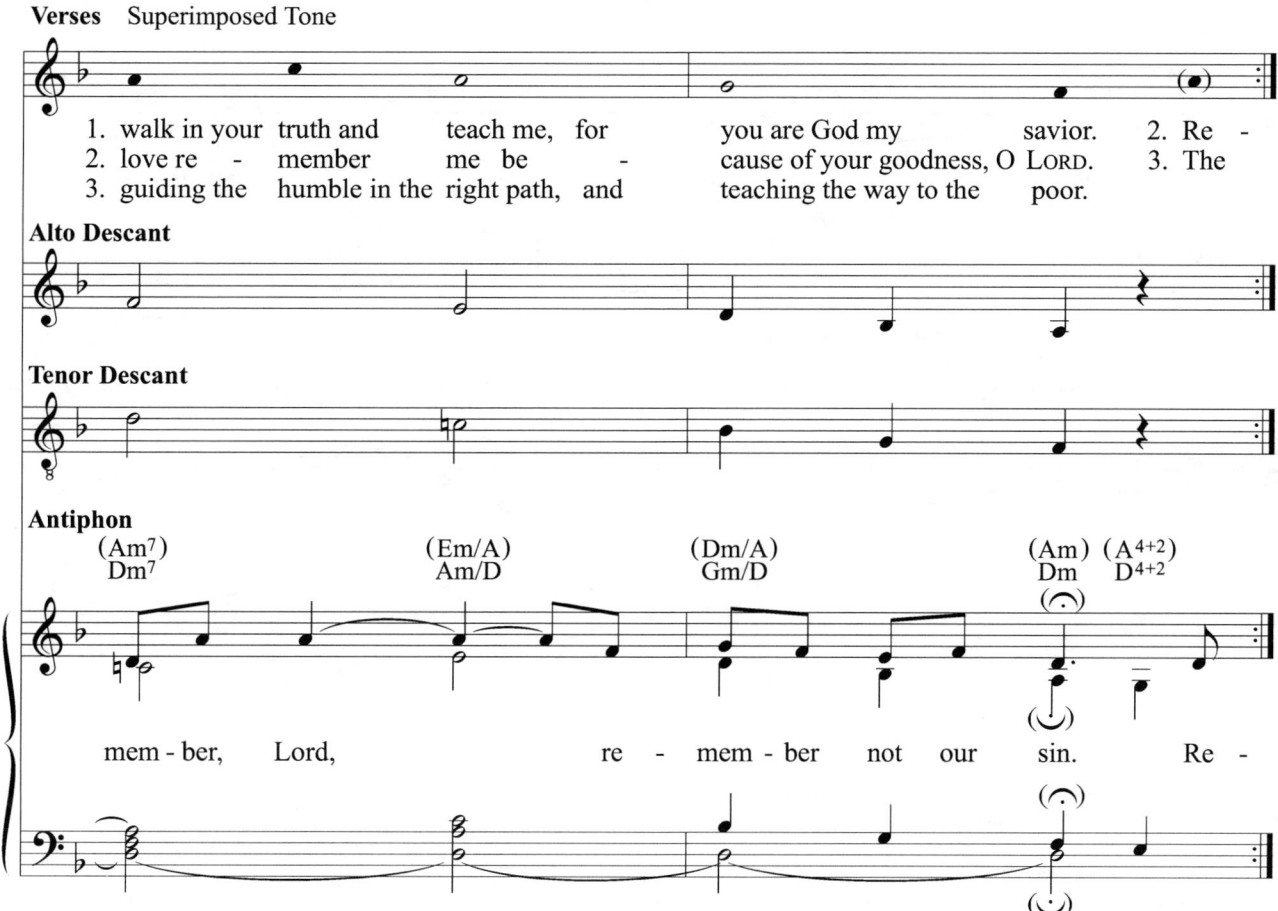

All That Is True

Twenty-seventh Sunday in Ordinary Time, Year A: Song for the Table

Verse Tone

Psalm 122

1. I rejoiced when I heard them say:
   "Let us go to God's house."
   And now our feet are standing
   *within your gates, O Jerusalem.

2. Jerusalem is built as a city
   strongly compact.
   It is there that the tribes go up,
   the tribes of the Lord.

3. For Israel's law it is,
   *there to praise the Lord's name.
   There were set the thrones of judgement
   *of the house of David.

4. For the peace of Jerusalem pray:
   "Peace be to your homes!
   May peace reign in your walls,
   in your palaces, peace!"

5. For love of my fam'ly and friends
   *I say: "Peace upon you."
   For the love of the house of the Lord
   I will ask for your good.

Performance Notes

Use the small cue-size notes (second measure of the verse tone) on the verse lines marked with an asterisk.

The antiphon may be sung as suggested with the cantor leading and the assembly responding to each phrase. Another option is to divide the assembly into two groups, with one group leading and the other responding (women in one group, men in the other or right side of the church in one group, left side in the other).

The Antiphon melody is the old English folk melody "O Waly, Waly."

Psalm text: The Grail (England), © 1963, 1986, 1993, 2000, The Grail, GIA Publications, Inc., agent. All rights reserved. Used with permission.
Antiphon melody: O WALY WALY, LM; English; arrangement, verse tone and antiphon text: © 2007, The Collegeville Composers Group. All rights reserved.
Published and administered by the Liturgical Press, Collegeville, MN 56321.

I Shall Dwell in the House of the Lord

Twenty-eighth Sunday in Ordinary Time, Year A: Song for the Word

Psalm 23

1. LORD, you are <u>my</u> shepherd;
   there is nothing I shall want.
   Fresh and green are <u>the</u> pastures
   where you give <u>me</u> repose.

2. Near restful waters <u>you</u> lead me,
   to revive my drooping spirit.
   You guide me along the <u>right</u> path;
   you are true <u>to</u> your name.

3. If I should walk in the valley <u>of</u> darkness
   no__ evil would I fear.
   You are there with your crook and <u>your</u> staff;
   with these you <u>give</u> me comfort.

4. You have prepared a banquet <u>for</u> me
   in the sight__ of my foes.
   My head you have anointed <u>with</u> oil;
   my cup is <u>o</u>verflowing.

5. Surely goodness and kindness <u>shall</u> follow me
   all the days__ of my life.
   In the LORD's own house shall <u>I</u> dwell
   for <u>ev</u>er and ever.

Performance Notes
In measure 2 of the tone, extension lines in the text show where to observe the dotted slurs.

Psalm text: The Grail (England), © 1963, 1986, 1993, 2000, The Grail, GIA Publications, Inc., agent. All rights reserved. Used with permission.
Music and antiphon text: © 2007, The Collegeville Composers Group. All rights reserved. Published and administered by the Liturgical Press, Collegeville, MN 56321.

The Word of God at Work in Us

Thirty-first Sunday in Ordinary Time, Year A: Song for the Table

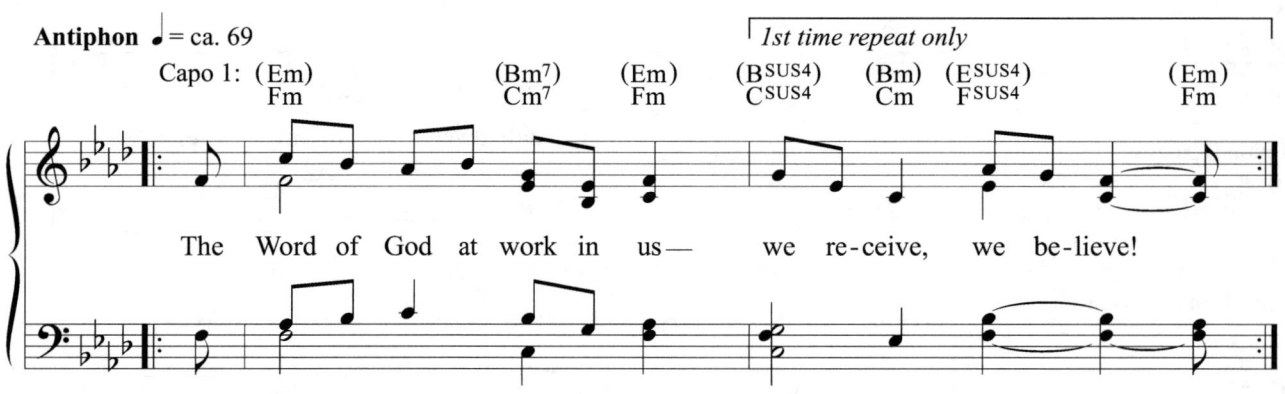

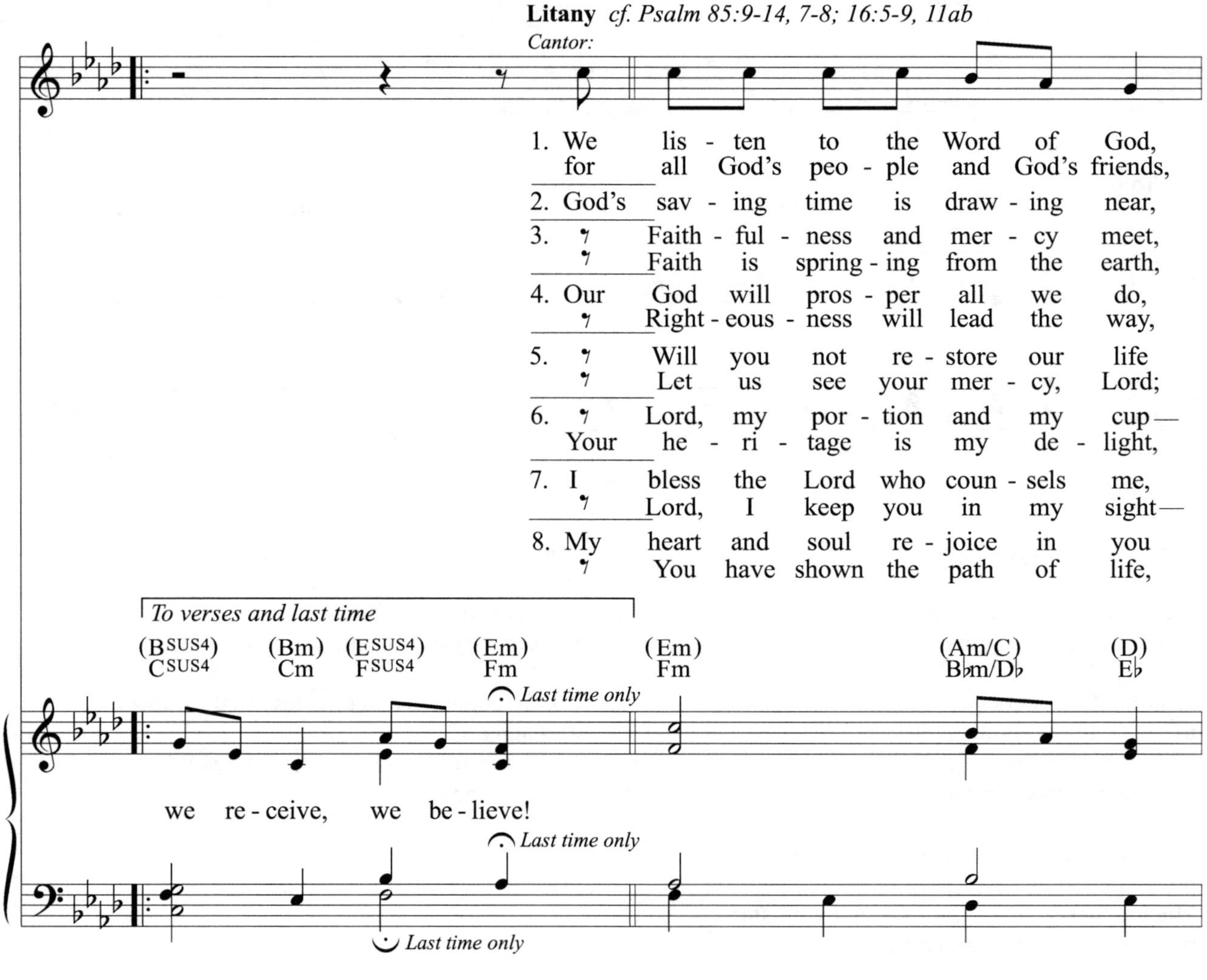

The Word of God at Work in Us, pg. 2

Come, All You Good and Faithful Servants
Thirty-third Sunday in Ordinary Time, Year A: Song for the Table

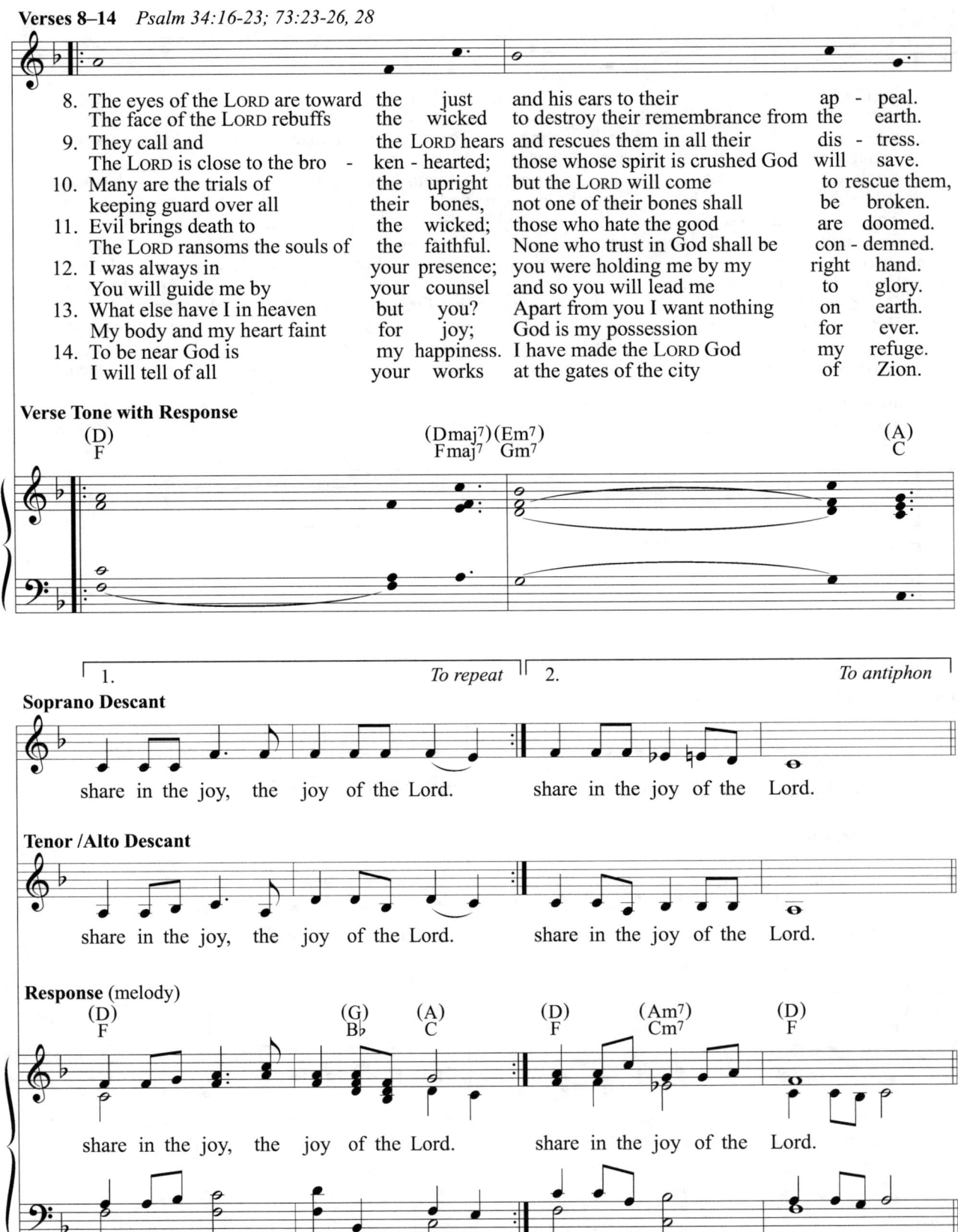

A River Flows

The Dedication of the Lateran Basilica, Years ABC: Song for the Word

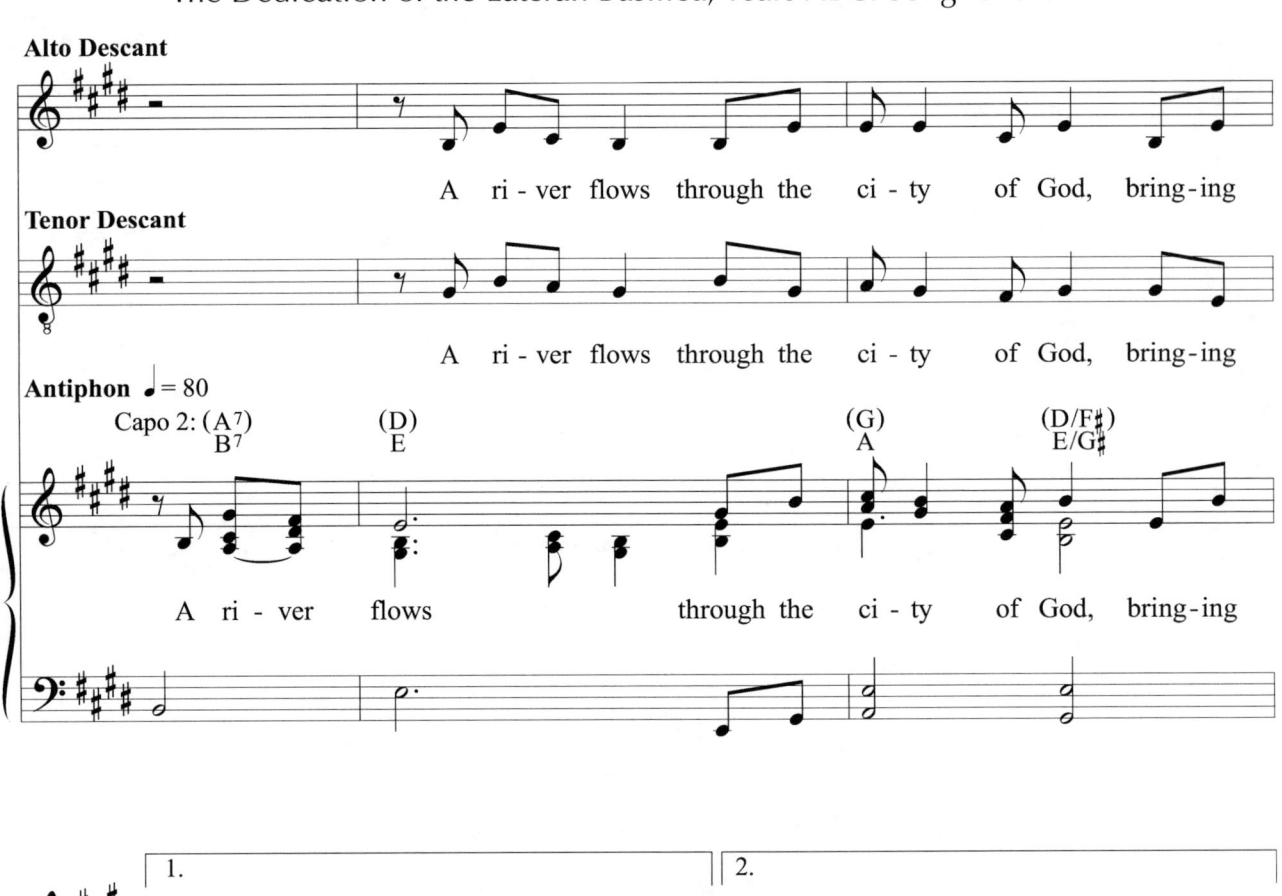
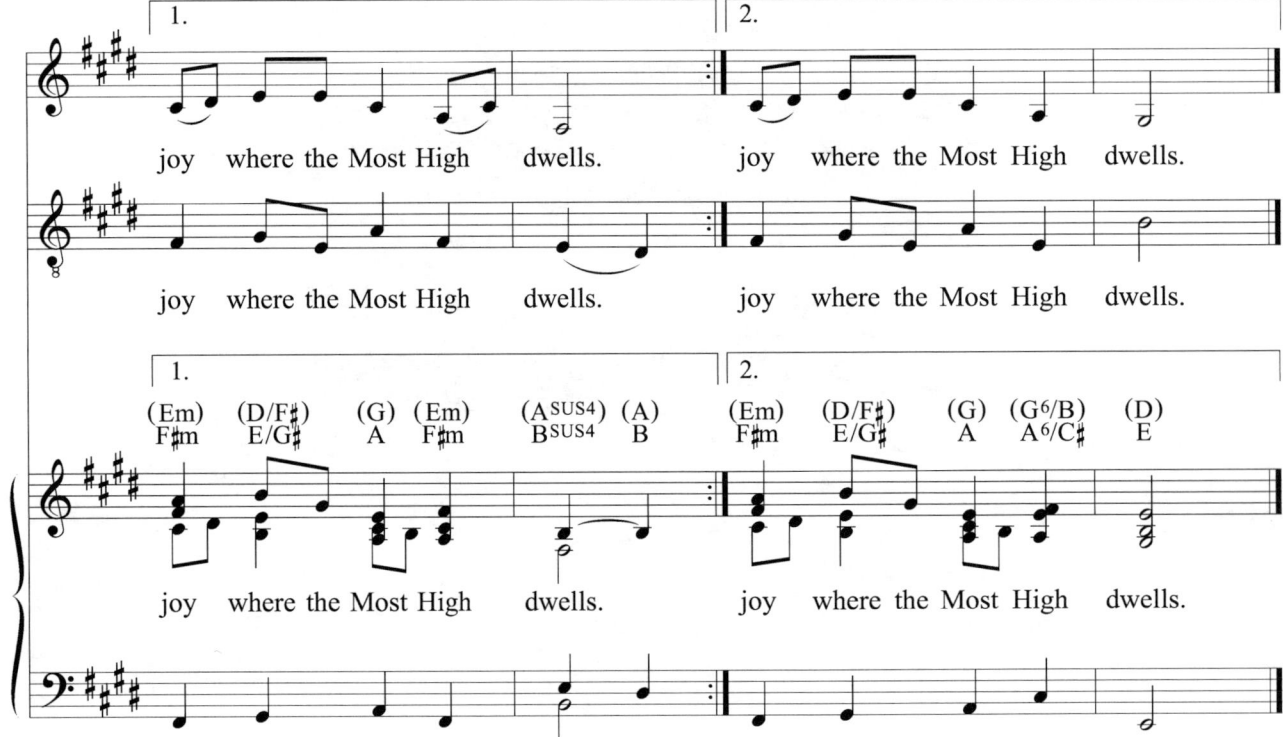

Verse Tone

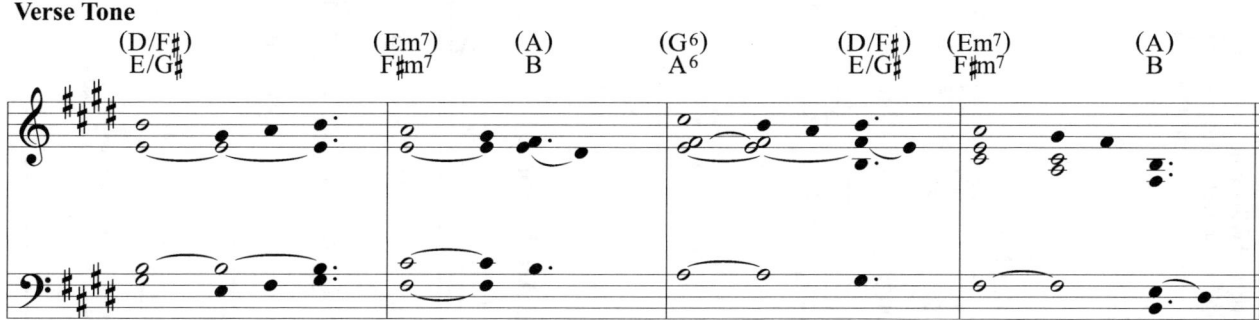

Psalm 46:2-3, 5-6, 11-12

1. God is for us a re<u>fuge</u> and strength,
   a helper close at hand, in time of <u>distress</u>,
   so we shall not fear though the <u>earth</u> should rock,
   though the mountains fall into the depths <u>of</u> the sea.

2. The waters of a river give joy <u>to</u> God's city,
   the holy place where the Most <u>High</u> dwells.
   God is within, it ca<u>nnot</u> be shaken;
   God will help it at the dawning <u>of</u> the day.

3. "Be still and know that <u>I</u> am God,
   supreme among the nations, supreme on <u>the</u> earth!"
   The Lord of <u>hosts</u> is with us;
   the God of Jacob <u>is</u> our stronghold.

Psalm text: The Grail (England), © 1963, 1986, 1993, 2000, The Grail, GIA Publications, Inc., agent. All rights reserved. Used with permission.
Music and antiphon text: © 2005, The Collegeville Composers Group. All rights reserved. Published and administered by the Liturgical Press, Collegeville, MN 56321.

Reprint Policy

Before reproducing the assembly graphics on pages 58–64, you must secure the appropriate Reprint License. By using this copyrighted material, you have a moral obligation to the composers whose livelihood depends on receiving a fair compensation for the use of their work. We trust that you value their work and will agree to this requirement. The following Reprint License options are available: 1) the purchase of a $35.00 Annual Reprint License from Liturgical Press (the reporting of titles is not required when reproduced; 2) membership with the licensing service OneLicense.net (you must report the use of titles each time they are reproduced). Each reprint must include the title and the full copyright notice as it appears below the graphic.

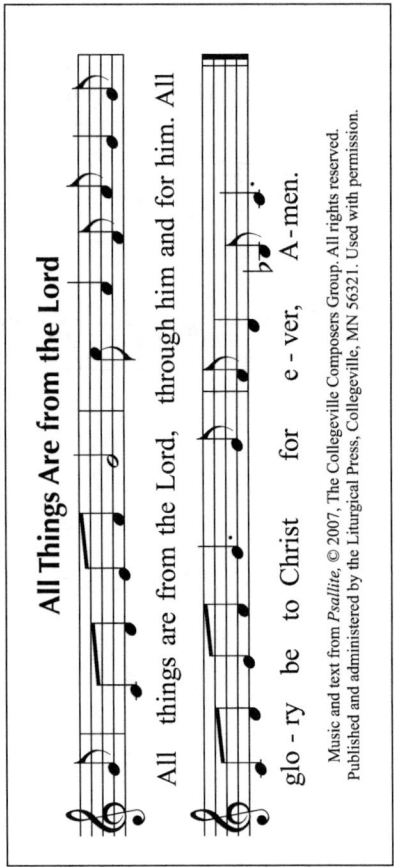

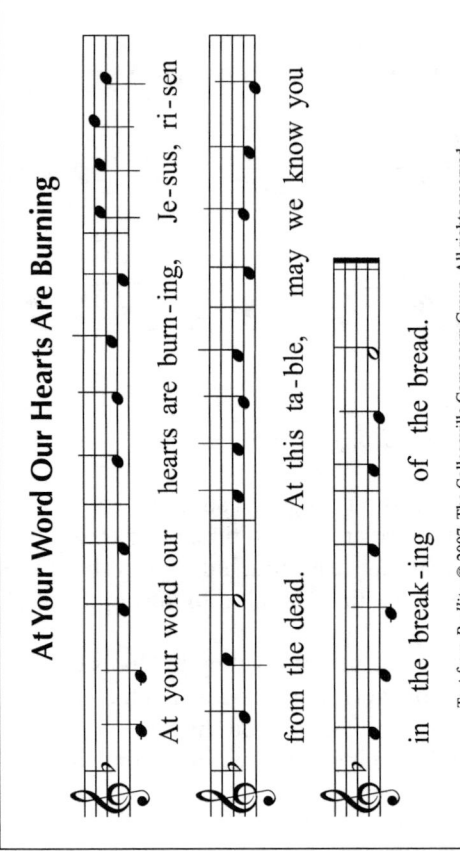

See page 58 for reprint policy.

See page 58 for reprint policy.

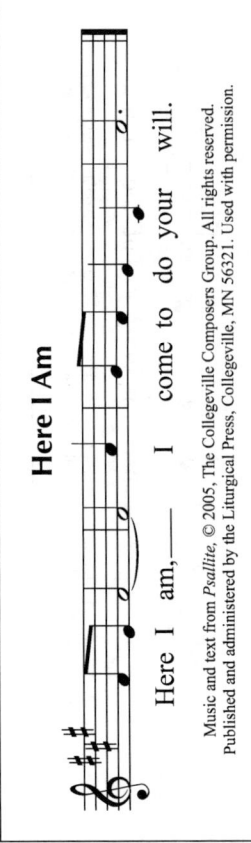
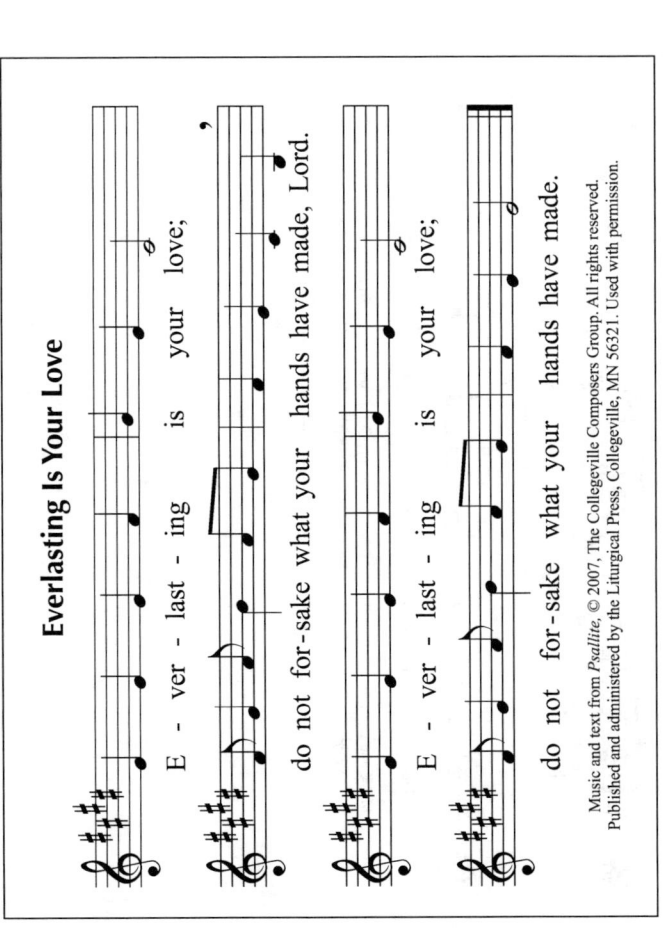
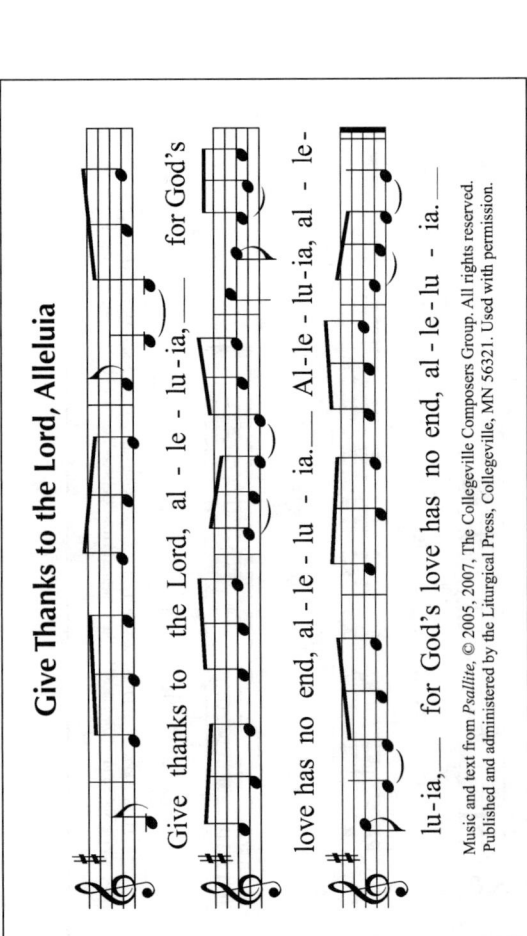

See page 58 for reprint policy.

61

See page 58 for reprint policy.

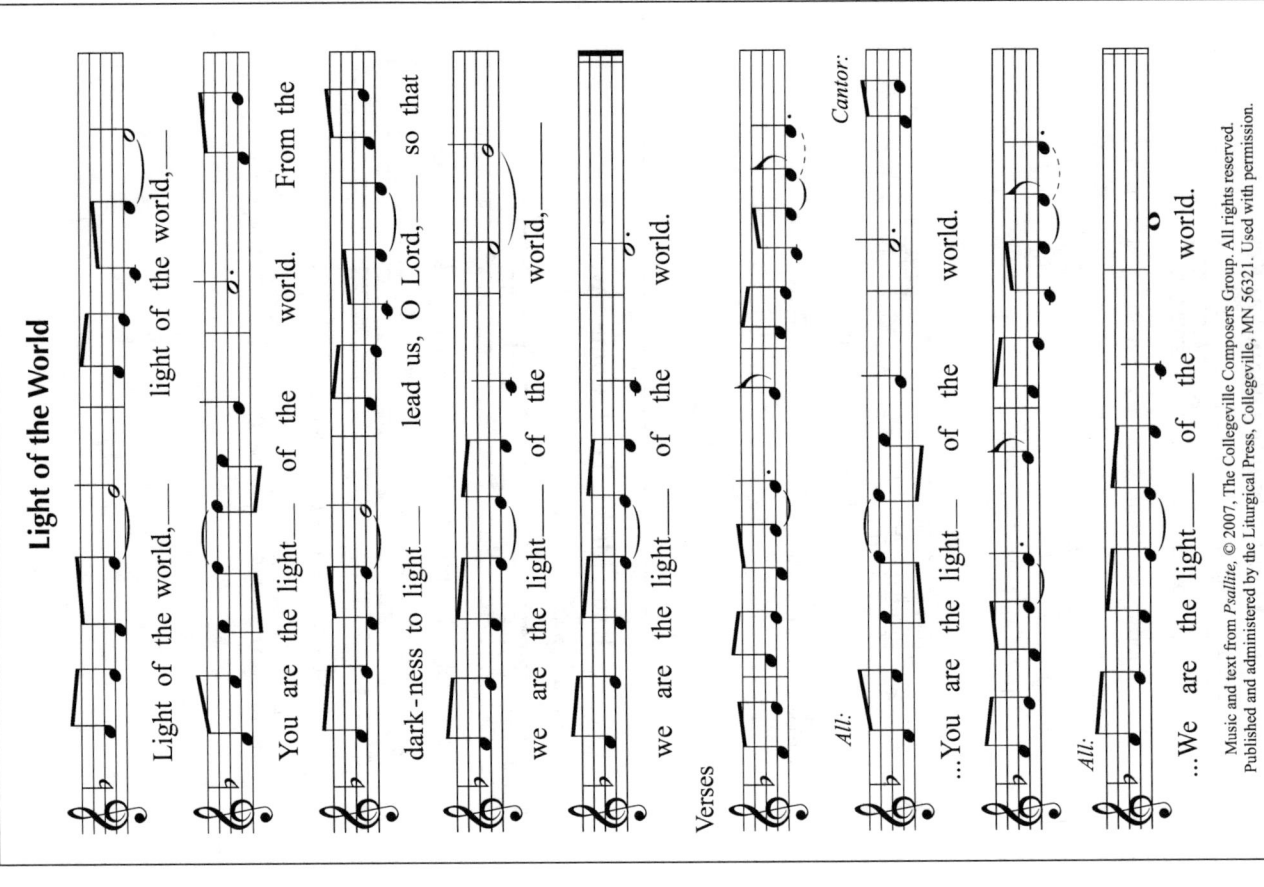

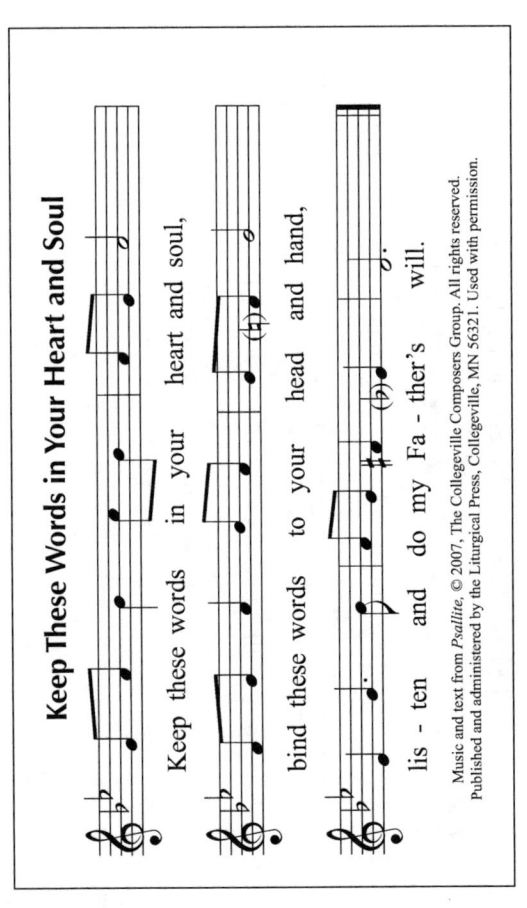

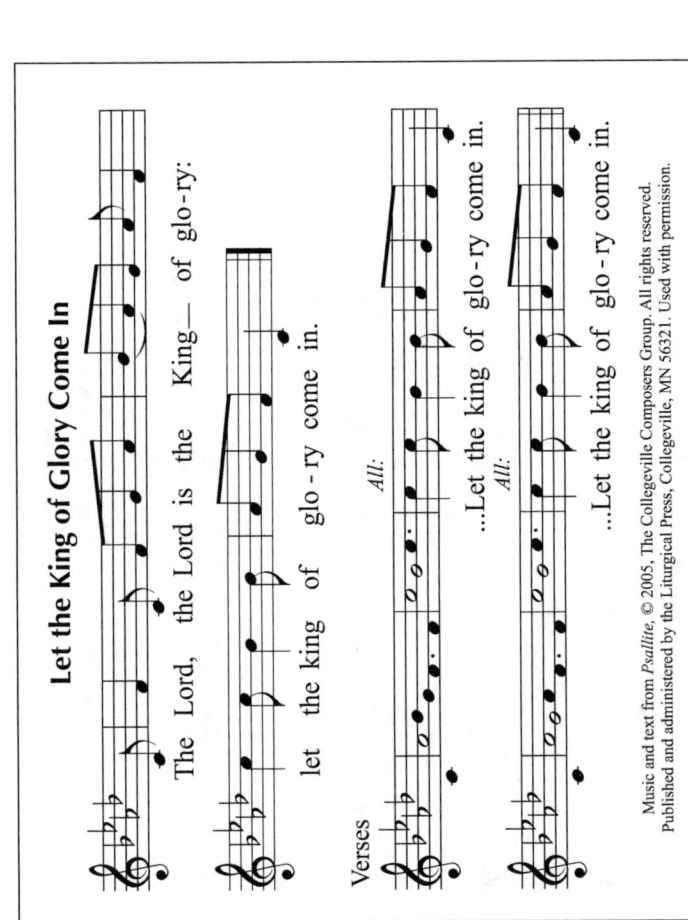

See page 58 for reprint policy.

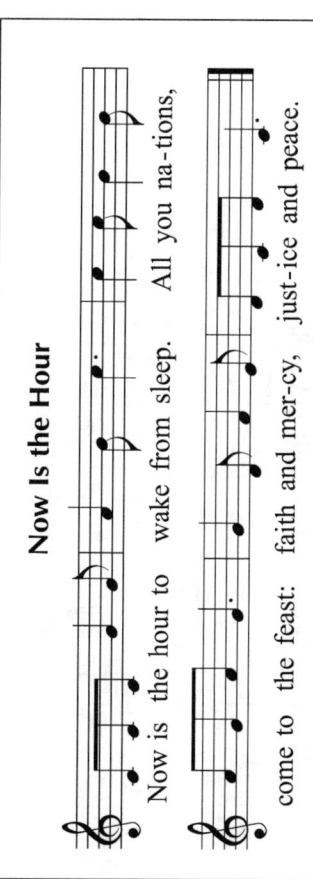

64

See page 58 for reprint policy.

Where Two or Three Are Gathered

Where two or three are ga-thered, ga-thered in my name, there am I, there am I in the midst of them.

Music and text from *Psallite*, © 2007, The Collegeville Composers Group. All rights reserved. Published and administered by the Liturgical Press, Collegeville, MN 56321. Used with permission.

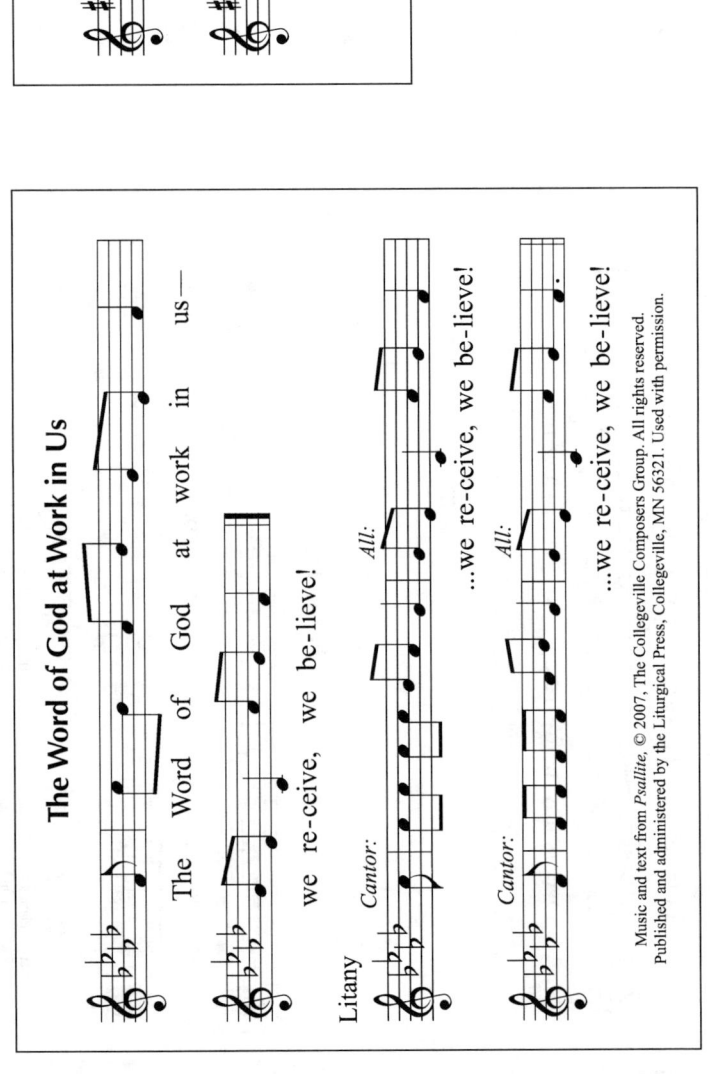

The Word of God at Work in Us

The Word of God at work in us— we re-ceive, we be-lieve!

Litany
Cantor: ... *All:* ...we re-ceive, we be-lieve!
Cantor: ... *All:* ...we re-ceive, we be-lieve!

Music and text from *Psallite*, © 2007, The Collegeville Composers Group. All rights reserved. Published and administered by the Liturgical Press, Collegeville, MN 56321. Used with permission.